D1388187

Embroidery
for the Church

Embroidery for the Church

Pat Beese

A Studio Handbook
Studio Vista

Acknowledgements

I wish to thank all those who have permitted me to use photographs of their work in this book. In particular, I would like to thank Mr A. N. Fairbairn, Director of Education for Leicestershire, who has given permission for me to use some work from an ecclesiastical project organized by the county for Loughborough Parish Church; Mr Edward Sharp, Principal of Loughborough College of Art and Design, for allowing me to use some of the students' work; Mr Ralph Downing, Head of the Department of Textiles/Fashion, Manchester Polytechnic, for permitting me to use some of his students' work, and Miss Anne Butler, Head of the Embroidery School at Manchester Polytechnic, who very kindly assisted in obtaining photographs of their work; Miss Ruth Elsey, Head of the Embroidery Department, Trent Polytechnic, who provided some work for photographs; Mr Alan Gregson, Dean of Mohawk College of Applied Arts and Technology, Hamilton, Ontario, who went to a great deal of trouble to provide me with photographs of some very exciting work which I saw when I visited Canada; and last but not least, photographers Mr Eric Gell, who took most of the photographs in this book, Terry Waddington and Stephen Yates.

Note: throughout the text the term 'baste' is used in the sense of 'tack'.

Studio Vista, a division of
Cassell and Collier Macmillan Publishers Limited
35 Red Lion Square, London WC1 4SG
an affiliate of Macmillan Inc., New York

ISBN 0 289 70531 2

Printed in Great Britain at
The Optima Press, Leicester

Contents

Foreword

Much of the ecclesiastical embroidery left by our forbears is now in a sad state of repair, and does not make the impact today that it must have made when it was produced. Many of our old, established churches are therefore in need of new furnishings and vestments. Modern churches are being built and they too require some adornment. The new order of service for the Church of England has changed the type of furnishings and vestments required, as well as the positioning of decoration on them. Consequently, recent years have seen an upsurge of interest in embroidery for the Church.

Purchased through normal channels – either from a professional designer or a church furnisher – vestments and furnishings can be very expensive and are often beyond the reach of many churches. However, quite a few churches have a group of women who meet regularly to repair vestments and to make small items for their church. Many other churches have amongst their members women who have sufficient interest and skill to produce some embroidery for the church, but who are often afraid to try. This neglected potential can be largely attributed to ignorance of the requirements and possibilities, and simple lack of self-confidence.

During recent years many efforts have been made by designers to produce embroidery of an up-to-date nature for the Church. There is scope for much more to be done but unfortunately many people are not sufficiently familiar with modern embroidery and the methods used to achieve it. This book is designed to help everyone wishing to produce some embroidery for their church and to encourage them to look at each project in a lively and modern way, instead of merely echoing the past.

1 The Historical Background

Although this book does not intend to follow past traditions, a brief history of ecclesiastical embroidery may help the reader to understand how the present situation has developed.

Christianity was adopted as the official religion of the Roman Empire with the conversion of Constantine during the fourth century A.D. Prior to this, Christians had been persecuted for their beliefs and consequently practised their religion in utmost secrecy. In order to express their religion they adopted pagan symbols, giving them a new significance; consequently, the first artistic expression of Christianity tends towards abstract design involving the use of these symbols.

Towards the end of the fourth century the use of pictures to illustrate and teach Christianity was introduced and from that time ecclesiastical buildings and objects of religious significance were decorated with scenes from the Old and New Testaments.

Church vestments developed naturally from the clothes which were in everyday use during the period of the establishment of Christianity and were therefore based on Roman dress of the third and fourth centuries. Christians felt that a uniform type of dress was necessary for officiating clergy and, although it took some time to establish, an official style was finally adopted. Gradually, the origins of the vestments were forgotten as fashions in ordinary clothes changed, and the vestments consequently took on a more symbolic significance.

It is difficult to estimate when ecclesiastical embroidery first appeared in Northern Europe, but there are existing examples from Anglo-Saxon times which have a high standard of technique. This suggests that the art was fairly well established when they were produced. It is possible that embroidery was developed during this period as a cheap substitute for the precious woven silks from Asia and the Near East.

Standards progressed considerably during the Middle Ages, especially in England, and it is doubtful whether any English art form has achieved such a widespread reputation as that of the ecclesiastical embroidery produced then. During the thirteenth and fourteenth centuries in particular Opus Anglicanum, as this excellent work came to be known, was sought after throughout Europe.

Contrary to popular belief these medieval embroideries were not produced by princesses and ladies of leisure entombed in their castles, but by skilled men in professional workshops, mostly in London. The production of Opus Anglicanum was a highly organized business with its own trade union, the Broderers' Guild.

At its best, the work they produced has never been surpassed in either design or craftsmanship. Most of it was carried out in silk and silver-gilt thread and it was often enriched with pearls and precious stones. It had a close relationship to jewellery and was often very valuable when finished – a sound investment for the merchants of the City of London. Church vestments now became symbols of wealth and power.

During the twelfth century ecclesiastical embroidery had a solemn, rather static appearance. The vestments were worked almost entirely in gold on silk backgrounds, usually of a sombre colour. The backgrounds were stitched with silk and not of silk fabric. Animals or human figures were often contained within rectangles, circles or round-headed arches which were decorated with ornamental foliage.

In the thirteenth century designs became more graceful and the drawing more naturalistic. Silk threads in natural colours were used for details such as hands and faces and the areas of gold work had chevron patterns instead of the brick patterns of the preceding century. The international reputation of English work grew immensely during the reign of Henry III; the Clare chasuble is one of the best examples of the embroidery of this period.

A much richer style developed during the reign of Edward I. The figures were elegant and were placed on backgrounds of gold or red silk as can be seen in the Vatican, Salzburg and Jesse copes.

The combined reigns of Edward II and Edward III roughly coincide with the decorated period of Gothic architecture, and the so-called East Anglian manuscripts. During this period Opus Anglicanum reached its summit. At first the designs were based on an arrangement of scenes contained within quatre-foils as can be seen in the Syon and Steeple Aston copes. Later these were followed by an opening out of the design in the form of concentric arcades as can be seen in the Bologna and Pienza copes.

Velvet came into fashion as a background during this period. The embroidery was worked on it through a thin piece of cloth on which the design was drawn. This was laid on the pile to make it easier to stitch.

From the middle of the fourteenth century a more restrained style related to perpendicular architecture began to manifest itself. The figures were more rigid and less lifelike in form. Some parts of the figures were occasionally raised and padded, which marked a departure from earlier work, when form was suggested by the direction of the stitch.

The Black Death and the wars at the end of the fourteenth century plunged England into social and economic stress and consequently the arts suffered. This put an end to Opus Anglicanum as such. Quantities of ecclesiastical embroidery were still produced and exported but it had lost the dynamic vitality of the earlier work. The designs tended to follow current fashions in Europe rather than setting the standard as hitherto.

Richly patterned Italian silk brocades and velvets were now being used throughout Europe for vestments and embroidery consequently played a lesser role in the design. It tended to be restricted to applied orphreys which were embroidered on linen. Designs became very stereotyped and certain subjects, such as scenes from the life of the Virgin and the Crucifixion, were standard.

During the fifteenth century it became the practice to embroider separate motifs and then cut them out and apply them to rich backgrounds of silk and velvet. This gave the design a scattered effect. It also became quite common to incorporate the coat of arms or even a portrait of the donor. In earlier times this was quite unheard of and was indicative of a move towards a more secular society.

Much of the ecclesiastical embroidery produced in the Middle Ages has not survived the centuries and a great deal was cut up and used for secular purposes during the Reformation.

Sixteenth-century embroidery was completely different in character and concept from medieval work. Very little ecclesiastical work was produced at this time but biblical scenes, especially Old Testament scenes, were often portrayed in secular embroidery, particularly on book covers. Many of these beautiful objects have great charm but they do not portray the religious zeal of earlier periods. This particular aspect of embroidery was much admired as pure decoration and continued into the seventeenth century in the form of panels using canvas stitches and stump work.

There was a brief revival of ecclesiastical embroidery in England in the early seventeenth century, under the auspices of Archbishop Laud. He reacted against the austerity of Puritanism and endeavoured to inspire a sense of richness and splendour in both church decoration and ritual. It is possible that some of the work was produced by professional embroiderers, although they were mainly engaged in secular work by this time.

After this period there was very little ecclesiastical embroidery produced until the nineteenth century, when many new churches were built in the Gothic revival style. This in turn stimulated a revival in medieval church embroidery. The movement was largely inspired by the architect Augustus

Pugin, who strongly condemned the embroidery being produced at the time as shallow and trivial in content, likening it to Valentine cards. He felt that people should look at medieval illuminated manuscripts, stained glass and particularly brasses for inspiration, and return to a heraldic use of colour. Pugin designed many sets of vestments and furnishings himself for his churches, and was the foremost innovator for the Catholic Church in this field.

The Anglican Church on the other hand was represented in the form of another architect, George Street. Street's sister and a friend, Miss Blencowe, founded the Ladies' Ecclesiastical Embroidery Society in 1854, the aim of which was to produce altar frontals either by reproducing old examples or by working under the supervision of an architect. Churches were charged for the cost of the materials only; the time and labour were given free.

G. F. Bodley was another nineteenth-century architect involved with embroidery design. He produced designs both for the Ladies' Ecclesiastical Embroidery Society and for his own churches. He was the first architect to commission Church work from the firm founded by William Morris and his associates.

William Morris had revolted against the machine-made articles of the time and also against the colours produced by chemical dyes. He endeavoured to return to the materials and methods of the Middle Ages and organized his firm accordingly. May Morris, his daughter, and the architect, Philip Webb, also produced designs for the Church. Lectern and pulpit falls, burses, offertory bags, chalice veils, and stoles were all embroidered in the firm's workshops.

Some of the most elaborate embroidery of the mid nineteenth century was designed by W. Curtis Brangwyn, the architect and designer. He had a workshop in Bruges and also designed for the London firm of Frank Smith and Co. Brangwyn's work had a contemporary flavour and tended to use sharp, angular forms more in keeping with the decorative arts of the period.

Art needlework also made its mark in the ecclesiastical as well as the domestic field during the 1870s. Many designs produced for art needlework could be adapted for ecclesiastical use. Frank Smith and Co. were inspired to produce a fabric known as Cluny tapestry. Their patterns were largely Gothic in character and the fabric was embroidered by hand in silk or crewel wools to produce hangings for churches. This work was carried out largely by women working at home and was usually made reversible by using a form of running stitch.

During the 1880s one of the leading English designers for Church embroidery was J. D. Sedding, who was appointed diocesan architect of Bath and Wells. His work was not based on historical formulae and had a naturalism and life which were not evident in other, more stylized works. Similar characteristics can be found in the work of Selwyn Image who was dismissed from the curacy in 1882 and from then on devoted all his time to designing.

By the end of the Victorian era, the differences between secular and ecclesiastical embroidery had diminished considerably. The treatment of ecclesiastical work had become much bolder and freer, using such techniques as appliqué in a striking manner.

With the passing of the Victorian age, enthusiasm for ecclesiastical embroidery again seems to have waned. It was not until after the Second World War that any significant work in this field was produced.

From that time onwards various well-known embroiderers have turned their attention to the Church and some very interesting work has resulted. Among the most outstanding of these must be Beryl Dean whose contribution both as an embroiderer and a teacher has done so much to stimulate and encourage Church embroidery throughout the world today.

2 Experimenting with Embroidery Techniques

Before you embark on a piece of ecclesiastical embroidery it is a good idea to experiment with a few techniques which you may want to incorporate in the final work. In order to make the best use of these experiments, forget the finished object and enjoy them for their own sake, taking each technique as far as possible without reference to practical problems. Work several techniques together rather than taking each one singly. Incorporate all your own ideas; the techniques and ideas described here are designed to inform and stimulate but do not constitute the only possibilities.

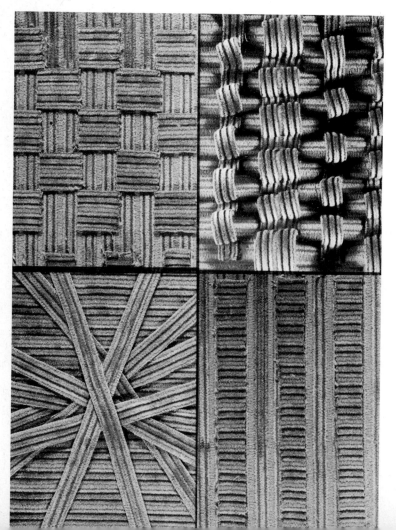

Fig. 1   Four samples showing various effects that can be obtained by cutting corded velvet. (Pat Beese)

Cutting, pleating and gathering

One of the most basic requirements for embroidery is an understanding of fabrics and what you can do with them. It is helpful to start by making a collection of bits of all the various types of fabric which are available. There are many exciting fabrics to be obtained if you search. Old fabrics can also be used for these experiments. Most people have a bit box, or if not, some old clothes which can be cut up and used. The main object is to collect as many different types of fabric as possible from rich, shiny satins, pile fabrics, including various types of velvet, to imitation fur, even odd bits of real fur, brushed mohair, and so on. Collect as many patterned fabrics as you can: various types of printed material, decorative weaves, such as jacquards, simple twill and herringbone. Don't forget knitted fabrics, plastics, rough tweeds, hessian (burlap), transparent organzas and chiffon. The variety is endless if you take the trouble to look.

When you have collected enough fabrics try a series of experiments with each one in order to observe how it behaves and what effects can be obtained from it.

The first and most obvious experiment is fraying. This is usually regarded as an undesirable quality in a fabric, but it can be used to advantage in a decorative context. Take an example of each type of fabric and fray it until there is at least $\frac{1}{4}$ inch (6 mm) of exposed thread; you can expose a great deal more but you are unlikely to see a good effect until at least this amount has been frayed (fig. 2). Some fabrics will now take on a new look, particularly where the warp threads are a different colour from those of the weft, or perhaps a different texture. Discard the fabrics that do not look interesting when frayed and try further experiments with those that seem to have possibilities. This might take the form of cutting the frayed fabric into strips and placing a series of strips one above the other, so that the frayed edges take on the appearance of a series of fringes (fig. 3). Both edges of the fabric can be frayed and used in a number of ways.

The look of a material can also be transformed by removing threads from areas within the fabric instead of from the edges. The best way to do this is with a pin; pick up individual threads with the tip of the pin and then pull them, either removing them completely or cutting them wherever you like (fig. 4). By this technique a plain piece of fabric can be transformed into a lacy one, with either a regular pattern or a more haphazard appearance, where threads have been only partially removed. Superimpose the result on another fabric or ribbons, or thread the fabric with strips of another fabric or thread. Groups of threads can be tied together to create larger holes. The design possibilities of this technique are endless.

Many interesting effects can be obtained by cutting fabrics. First, cut them into squares of equal size, and then place them

Fig. 2

Fig. 3

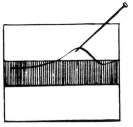

Fig. 4

together, touching each other, with the grain at right angles (fig. 5). This will have little effect on some fabrics, but others, such as velvet and all pile fabrics, shiny and patterned fabrics, should give interesting results. From these, shapes can be broken down even further, resulting in more complicated textures (see fig. 1).

Cut strips of fabric and weave them in and out of each other; loop them and change their directions. Bias strips placed next to strips cut on the straight can give exciting effects (fig. 6).

Pleating is another way of enhancing the quality of a fabric. The fabric may be pleated either on the straight grain or on the bias. The pleats can be of equal or unequal widths, according to the desired effect (fig. 7). Some transparent fabrics, as well as shiny and patterned fabrics, work well in this context.

Gathering (fig. 8) also gives interesting results. Many fabrics take on a completely new quality when gathered. Patterned fabrics can be distorted while shiny fabrics gain a greater depth. Some of the most exciting results are obtained when a number of rows of gathering stitches are used so that the fabric becomes ruched. This can be done by hand or using shirring elastic in the bobbin of a domestic sewing machine (fig. 9). When all the fabric has been gathered, finish off the ends and then push the gathers in different directions and sew them in position. This creates an interesting relationship between tightly gathered areas and relatively flat material.

Circular gathering can also be used. Instead of stitching straight across the fabric, stitch circles in either a regular or a haphazard fashion (fig. 10). They can be of equal size or they can be varied, according to the desired effect. This experiment can also be done with shirring elastic on the sewing machine. Concentric circles using this method produce fascinating effects, especially on slightly shiny fabrics.

Appliqué

Appliqué is the easiest and most obvious way of obtaining a shape in a piece of embroidery. Briefly, it is a shape in one fabric applied to another, usually a background fabric. There are three methods of achieving this and all of them have a slightly different appearance when finished.

The most straightforward method is to cut out the required shape and place it on the background fabric. However, it is not quite so simple as this. When applying one fabric to another, you must place the applied shape on the straight grain of the background fabric. The straight grain can be found by looking at the way a fabric has been woven. All woven fabrics have a warp and weft thread, which cross each other at right angles, no matter what pattern may appear on the surface (fig. 11). If you are in doubt – and it can be difficult for the inexperienced to ascertain the warp and the weft from some weave structures – fray a small corner to establish where

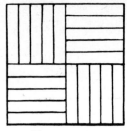

Fig. 5

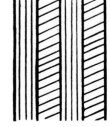

Fig. 6

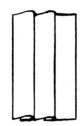

Fig. 7

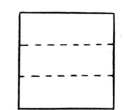

Fig. 8

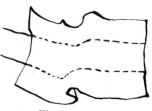

Fig. 9

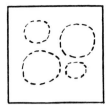

Fig. 10

Fig. 11

Fig. 12

the threads cross. The cross-grain or bias of a fabric is at 45°
to the warp and weft threads (fig. 12).

The bias has a special property, because cut at this angle a
fabric stretches considerably more than it does on the straight
grain; this is particularly important in dressmaking. However,
if you apply a fabric on the cross it is very likely to pucker, due
to this stretching property, which cannot always be eliminated.

A simple way of ensuring that a fabric is applied on the
straight grain is to make a tracing of the shape to be applied
and draw a straight line on the shape in a vertical position

Fig. 13 Some of the effects that
can be obtained by using shirring
elastic on a sewing machine.
(Pat Beese)

(fig. 14). Cut out the traced shape and use it as a pattern, placing the vertical line on the straight grain of the fabric. Cut out the shape and place it on the straight grain of the background fabric in the desired position. Pin it on carefully, ensuring that it is absolutely flat and being careful not to stretch it in any way. Baste (tack) the shape down. If it is large, place one or two rows of basting across the middle to ensure that it is held flat until it has been properly fixed; then baste around the outer edge (fig. 15). Do not attempt to sew the shape into position until all the applied shapes have been cut out and basted onto the background. This is because some shapes may overlap or be very close to others and it may be possible to fix them with one area of stitching rather than two.

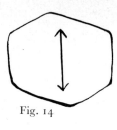

Fig. 14

When fixing an applied shape to a background you can treat the process of attaching it as decoration or as something to be done as invisibly as possible. The simplest method of fixing is to use a decorative embroidery stitch around the edge, such as couching. This, however, presents a rather dull effect, and it is much more interesting if the shape is held down by tiny stitches in a matching thread (fig. 16), so that they are as invisible as possible, and then embroidered in a free way over the top (fig. 17). By using this method, the applied shape becomes much more integrated with the embroidery. If the same stitch is used right around the edge, the shape tends to stand out too much and become isolated from the rest of the embroidery.

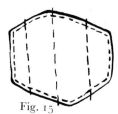

Fig. 15

The second method of appliqué is to turn a hem round the shape, instead of leaving raw edges, as in the previous method. This can only be used on simple shapes and gives a more raised look than flat appliqué. The pattern for the shape is made in exactly the same way as the previous method but when cutting the shape out of fabric allow $\frac{1}{4}$–$\frac{1}{2}$ inch (6–13 mm) extra for the hem, depending on the type of fabric (fig. 18). It is a good idea to baste round the edge of the pattern shape before cutting out; and the basting will then act as a guide line for the hem. Turn in a single hem around the shape along the basting. Where the shape is slightly curved, the edge will not be flat, so you will have to make a series of cuts around the edge almost to the basting. Sometimes it is necessary to remove small wedges of fabric, as there is too much in the hem (fig. 19). There will always be a considerable bulk of fabric at the corners; this should be cut away until only one layer remains, but be careful not to let the fabric fray too much.

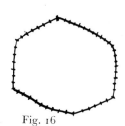

Fig. 16

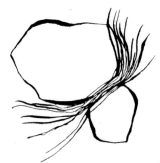

Fig. 17

When the cutting is complete, press the shape on the wrong side with an iron, and then place it in position on the background fabric. Pin and baste it down in exactly the same way as the first method. The shape should be sewn down as invisibly as possible by a small hem stitch in a matching thread (fig. 20). Large areas of appliqué are easier to fix by this method if they are stretched in a frame.

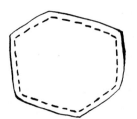

Fig. 18

16

Fig. 19

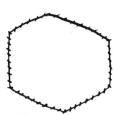

Fig. 20

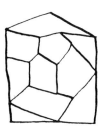

Fig. 21

Fig. 22

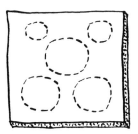

Fig. 23

The third method gives yet a different appearance. Strictly speaking, it is not true appliqué but inlay; nevertheless it is concerned with applying fabrics to a background. Much greater accuracy is required to give a satisfactory result with this method. You have to work this technique in a frame, although an embroidery ring is quite adequate for a small sample.

Inlay is made up of a number of small pieces of fabric which fit together, rather like a jigsaw or mosaic (fig. 21). A backing fabric, such as unbleached calico, is stretched in an embroidery ring and the pieces of fabric are cut so that they fit accurately together. They are then pinned to the calico and basted in position. When all the pieces are in position, they can be permanently fixed to the calico by the use of hand or machine embroidery, which can be decorative as well as functional.

Padding

Padding is used quite extensively in embroidery today and can produce interesting three-dimensional effects. There are four main types of padding in current use, each of which gives a slightly different appearance.

The first and simplest method gives an all-over padding and is formed by making a sandwich of the padding material between fabric to be padded and backing material (fig. 22).

There are many materials that can be used for padding and the final choice depends on the effect you want to obtain. If you are not familiar with these materials it is a good idea to experiment with all of them until you achieve satisfactory results. Cotton wadding is very cheap and can be obtained in black and white. It is only about $\frac{1}{3}$ inch (9 mm) thick and compresses very easily, giving only a slight padding. It can of course be used in several layers. Fleecy dommett also comes in black and white and has a similar effect. It has slightly more bounce than cotton wadding and therefore gives a different texture. Again, several layers can be used. Dacron is a much thicker padding and is made in various thicknesses, starting at approximately $\frac{1}{2}$ inch (13 mm) and going up to approximately $1\frac{1}{2}$ inches (38 mm). This is useful if you are trying to achieve a more raised effect.

All these padding materials become compressed when the fabric is stitched. The degree of compression varies according to the amount of stitching. This has to be taken into account when deciding on the quantity of padding you are going to use.

A backing material, such as unbleached calico, the same size as the material to be padded, is placed on a flat surface. Put the required amount of padding on top and cut to the size and shape of the fabric to be padded. Place the fabric in position on top of the padding. Pin the three layers together carefully and baste them together. Use decorative stitchery either by hand or machine to hold the layers together (fig. 23).

Stuffed quilting or trapunto gives a raised effect to certain areas only, leaving the background flat. A backing fabric, such as calico, the same size as the overall fabric to be embroidered, is again required. Place it on a flat surface and cover with the main fabric, making sure that the grains of the two fabrics are going the same way. Pin the fabrics together and baste firmly. Stitch the required shape either by hand or machine through the two layers (fig. 24). Turn the embroidery over and make a slit through the middle of the shape in the backing fabric only (fig. 25). A good pair of small, sharp, pointed scissors is the best instrument for this – but take great care not to cut the front. Stuff the shape with Dacron teased out, cotton wool, or a little combed fleece, if available. When the shape has sufficient padding, lace up the back with a needle and thread, so that the stuffing does not protrude (fig. 26).

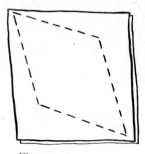

Fig. 24

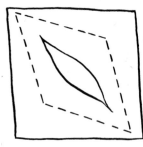

Fig. 25

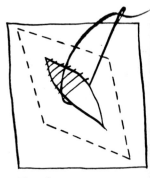

Fig. 26

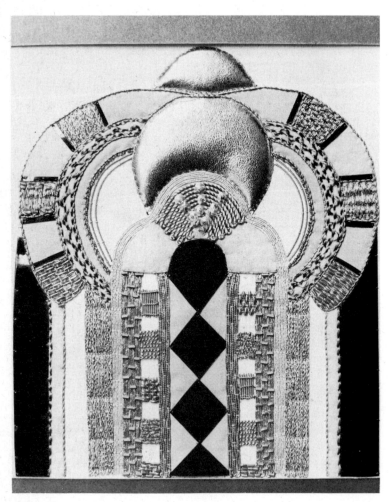

Fig. 27 Detail of motif on a white background with pale pink and greyish-green appliqué, acetate, padded gold kid and a variety of gold threads.
(Jean Bagguley)

18

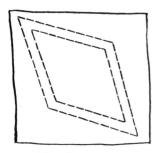

Fig. 28

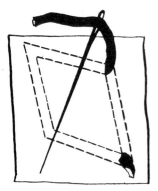

Fig. 29

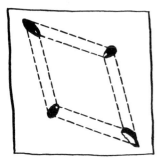

Fig. 30

Italian quilting is similar to trapunto but instead of producing a shape it gives a raised line. The fabric to be embroidered and the backing are basted together in exactly the same way as the method used in trapunto. When this process is complete, stitch the design which is formed from parallel lines approximately $\frac{1}{4}$ inch (6 mm) apart or less (fig. 28). Obviously, you can experiment with this technique, but remember that it would not be easy to work if the lines were more than 1 inch (25 mm) apart. Turn the fabric onto the reverse side and make a small hole in the backing fabric only, with a blunt-ended needle. Thread quilting wool or cord along the channel created by the parallel lines of stitching, cutting it at the end (fig. 29). When turning sharp points or corners, bring the thread out at the end of one angle and re-insert it in the next one, leaving a small loop of thread at the corner. This prevents the material from puckering (fig. 30).

Another method of padding which is used quite extensively in ecclesiastical embroidery is the one used for suède, leather and gold and silver kid. This is a more solid form of padding than the other techniques. Almost every shape of leather or suède requires some padding, as it never seems to lie flat if it

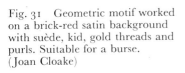

Fig. 31 Geometric motif worked on a brick-red satin background with suède, kid, gold threads and purls. Suitable for a burse. (Joan Cloake)

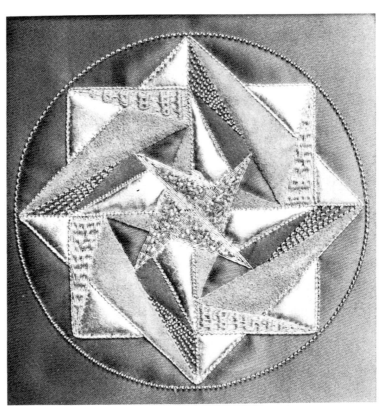

is just applied onto a piece of material. Felt is used for this method and it is built up in layers according to the height which the final shape will be raised from the fabric. Cut a felt shape about an $\frac{1}{8}$ inch (3 mm) smaller all round than the shape to be padded. If more layers are desired, cut them consecutively smaller. The colour of the felt does not matter particularly, as long as you take care when working it, because the felt should not show when the leather is applied. If this method is used for padding gold thread, however, then it would be advisable to use yellow felt.

To work this method, the fabric must be stretched in a frame, but for a sample an embroidery ring can again be used. Stretch a background fabric on a ring and place the smallest felt shape in the middle of the area to be padded. Hold it in place with basting stitches and then stitch around it with small stitches at right angles to the edge in a matching thread. Put the next piece on top, making sure that the small piece is in a central position. Stitch this layer down in the same way as the first one. Continue with this process until the final shape is fixed in position (fig. 32). It is very important that each piece of felt is sewn down firmly, otherwise it could shift when the article is in use.

Fig. 32

Now place the suède or leather in position over the top of the felt. In order to hold it in place while working, take a few large stitches right across the shape in opposite directions (fig. 33). Do not baste in the normal way, as your needle will puncture the leather. Choose a matching thread and as small a needle as possible and stitch around the leather shape in the same way as the felt, keeping the stitches approximately $\frac{1}{12}$ inch (2 mm) apart (fig. 34). The stitches should be as small as possible in order to keep the work looking neat, but take care not to split the leather. When working to produce a finished article it is advisable to wax the thread. This is done by drawing the thread across a piece of beeswax before you start stitching.

Fig. 33

Fig. 34

Simple experiments with stitches

Most people think only about the technical aspects of construction when considering embroidery stitches; the use of samplers to teach stitches encourages this attitude. Unfortunately, this method still persists and does nothing at all to promote the creative use of stitchery. It doesn't matter how many stitches you know; it is how they are used which is the important factor. An appreciation of the aesthetic qualities of various types of stitchery is extremely important for successful embroidery, and it is from this point of view that this section is written.

Stitching is done with thread, so it is important to choose the right type of thread for a particular stitch in a particular position, or the design will not work. There are thick threads, thin threads, threads with dull and shiny surfaces, rough

20

threads and smooth threads; altogether a very wide variety can be obtained. The number of threads manufactured specially for embroidery has decreased somewhat, unfortunately, but these can be substituted by many other types of yarn. Knitting yarns are an obvious addition, but it is also possible to buy a wide variety of weaving yarns. Oddments of unusual yarn can also be found from time to time if you keep your eyes open for them.

Before you actually start stitching it is a good idea to make a collection of as many different types of yarn as possible in order to exploit your stitchery to the full.

Stitchery is often used to produce a linear quality in a design, and this is perhaps one of its most important uses.

Fig. 35 Stitchery used to give a textural effect on a coarse uneven-weave linen. Various threads have been used, including rug yarn, tapestry wool, stranded cotton, soft embroidery cotton and weaving yarn.
(Enez Munton)

There are some stitches that cannot be used to produce a line under any circumstances because of their nature. These include canvas stitches, drawn and pulled thread stitches and filling stitches of various kinds. Some of these will be dealt with later but we are now concerned with the stitches that are produced in a single line.

If a few simple embroidery stitches, such as running stitch, back stitch, chain stitch, etc., are worked on a piece of fabric it is immediately obvious that each one produces a different type of line (fig. 36). Running stitch produces a thin, broken line, back stitch gives a thin, more or less continuous line, and chain stitch a thicker line with scalloped edges which catches the light when the fabric is moved.

It is possible to go through the whole range of linear embroidery stitches and discover that each one has a different quality. Some produce a thick, heavy line like heavy chain stitch and basket stitch (fig. 37); others have a heavy, but knobbly appearance, such as cable knotted chain (fig. 39) and raised chain band. Some stitches look almost like braid when they are worked, such as threaded herringbone and interlacing

Fig. 36

Fig. 37

Fig. 38 Detail of a thread construction over cut shapes on textured satin with a padded centre, using a variety of threads. (Maureen Curtis)

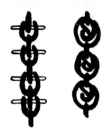

Fig. 39

Fig. 40

Fig. 41

stitch (fig. 40). Some stitches are more raised from the surface of the fabric than others.

The qualities of each stitch can be further exploited by the use of different yarns. The same stitch worked in a variety of threads will produce a surprising number of subtle variations. A stitch produced in one strand of stranded cotton gives a totally different type of line to the same stitch done in thick wool.

There are endless possibilities using linear stitches. One interesting experiment is to collect a variety of media, such as pencil, pen, wax crayon and charcoal, and make a series of designs fitting into small squares or rectangles, using a variety of lines derived from the various media. Positive changes in direction can add interest to the compositions as can a good variation between thick and thin lines (fig. 41). The variety of media gives different surface textures to the lines and lends the designs a great deal of interest.

Choose your most interesting design and try to interpret it in terms of linear stitches only, selecting stitches that will give the closest similarity both in width and texture to the line on paper. This should be enhanced by a careful selection of

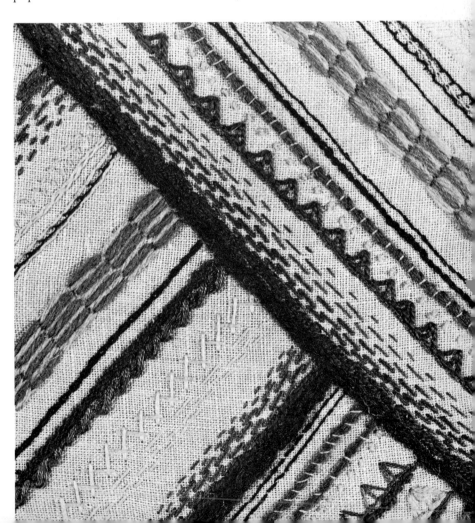

Fig. 42 Linear stitches with a strong change of direction. (Grace Kirkman)

threads, not only for width, but also surface texture, which also contributes to the quality of the stitch.

The type of composition described above indicates a fairly rigid approach to the execution of a stitch, following such principles as regularity in spacing, etc., but it is possible to treat linear stitches in an irregular way if a freer effect is desired (fig. 44). This is mainly achieved by the deliberate variation of the length or width of a stitch. The simplest example of this can be seen with running stitch and chain stitch.

Fig. 43 Sample showing a free use of linear stitches, which indicates some of the richness that can be obtained with this technique. (Enez Munton)

Fig. 44

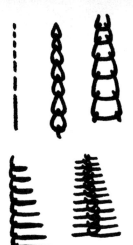

Fig. 45

Fig. 46

Fig. 47

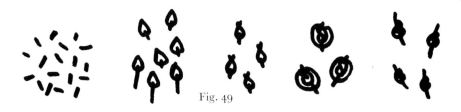

Fig. 48

Open chain stitch can be varied in both length and width at the same time. This is also possible with a number of other stitches, such as blanket stitch and Cretan stitch (fig. 45).

It is not possible to vary all linear stitches in this way as some, like interlacing stitch and raised chain band, rely on fairly rigid spacing for their actual construction. Nevertheless, a great many stitches can be varied to produce some interesting effects. However, don't forget that there is a difference between variation in spacing and bad technique. One is deliberate, the other is not, and it is easy to distinguish between the two.

Stitches can be done on top of each other and they can be made to cross over. Many exciting effects can be gained by producing more designs in a similar way to your first one, but making the lines freer, and then interpreting them in terms of stitchery.

Texture
Texture is another important factor in design. There are several stitches that will produce a texture, rather than a line. Most of these are classed as filling stitches. However, there are other stitches, such as French knots, that do not fit strictly in either category. A French knot is very rarely done as a single stitch. Most people group them together, either very closely, as can be seen in some Chinese embroideries, or spaced slightly apart (fig. 46). Either way, a texture rather than a line is produced. This can also be done with bullion knots, fly stitch (fig. 47) or spider's web.

Texture can also be derived from line stitches. The simplest method is to work several rows of the same stitch side by side, e.g. running stitch and chain stitch (fig. 48). These build up to become an area of texture rather than a line. It is possible to build up freer areas of texture by using line stitches singly and placing them in a random fashion. The most familiar form of this is a single chain stitch or lazy daisy, but the same thing can be done with a number of stitches, e.g. running stitch, twisted chain, cable knotted chain or double knot stitch (fig. 49).

An interesting exercise in texture can be evolved from cutting out small areas of texture from magazine advertisements and putting them together in a collage, either in an abstract composition or as a representative image. The composition can then be interpreted in terms of stitchery. It is a good idea to keep the size quite small at this stage, as it can take a long time to work.

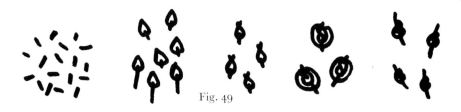

Fig. 49

Machine embroidery

Hitherto machine embroidery has been little used in ecclesiastical embroidery but there is no reason why it should not now be incorporated. Many interesting effects can be obtained simply using the domestic machine. You do not need to have a fully automatic machine which produces the so-called embroidery stitches in order to do machine embroidery. However, a zigzag stitch is very useful.

Fig. 50   Letter S, using covered washers with shisha glass behind, together with French knots in a variety of threads and beads. (Brenda Marchbank)

Fig. 51   A burse of an unusual shape designed for a country church. The embroidery has almost all been done by machine and enriched with some beads. (Katherine Shaw)

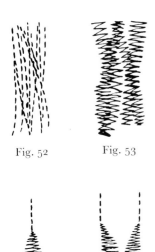

Fig. 52   Fig. 53

Fig. 54 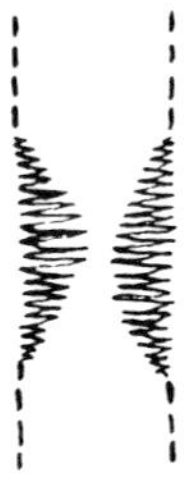   Fig. 55

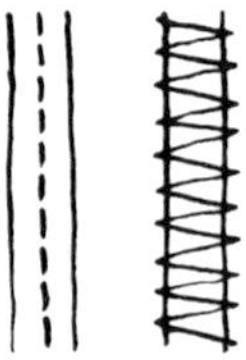

Fig. 56

Fig. 57.

If the machine is a modern one and has a reverse, surprisingly free textures can be obtained by using the machine as set up for ordinary dressmaking. Machine a row forwards in straight stitching and press the reverse button, making a line almost the same length as the forward one. You will soon find that it is very difficult to keep the reverse line exactly on the forward one. So make use of this and by turning the fabric produce a texture built up from the rows of machining (fig. 52). The same thing can be done with the zigzag stitch, and as you can vary the widths and degrees of openness you can achieve quite a variety in the weight of texture (fig. 53).

Decorative effects can also be obtained by switching from straight stitching to zigzag, as well as by opening and closing the stitch (fig. 54).

If the machine has a zigzag stitch, there should also be a lever for the needle position. Normally, the needle is left in the central position, but if it is moved either to the right or left, the stitching will build up on that side (fig. 55).

Thicker threads can be applied by machine instead of being couched by hand. This can be done either by straight machining through the middle of the thread or zigzagging over it (fig. 56). Use can also be made of the reverse stitch in order to give a freer or heavier appearance to some areas. Threads can be applied in a free way by placing a bunch of them on the fabric and machining over it in a free manner with either straight stitching or zigzag, or a mixture of both (fig. 57).

A much wider variety of line and texture can be obtained by the methods usually referred to as free machine embroidery. You will find this possible on almost every domestic machine, irrespective of its age, provided it is possible to remove the presser foot and lower the feed or teeth. In order to obtain satisfactory results, the fabric must be stretched in an embroidery ring. The ring should not be more than about 8 inches (20 cm) in diameter in order to achieve the best manipulation. It is very important that the fabric is evenly stretched because any slackness will prevent the machine from stitching properly. The grain of the fabric should not be distorted.

Remove the presser foot, lower the feed and try some simple experiments with the machine. Place the embroidery ring under the needle, making sure that the needle is not too near the edge. Put the lever that normally operates the presser foot down in order to obtain the correct pressure. If this is not done, the machine will not stitch correctly. Bring the bottom thread up through the fabric by turning the wheel and hold the top and bottom threads for a few seconds when you start stitching.

Because the feed has been lowered, you are now in complete control of the machine and will have to move the embroidery ring in order to obtain a row of stitching. The stitch length is determined by the speed at which the ring is moved. The ring can be moved in any direction but in order to get the feel of

Fig. 58   Detail of fig. 155 which shows the direction of the machine embroidery. (Beryl Patten)

Fig. 59

Fig. 60

Fig. 61

the technique it is best to start with simple backwards and forwards movements, endeavouring to get the stitches of equal length, so that you have some degree of control over what is happening (fig. 59). Try building up a variety of textures using this movement.

When you have acquired sufficient confidence explore the possibilities of circular movements, which require rather more control. Experiment with textures using this movement (fig. 60).

Free machine embroidery can also be done using the zigzag stitch. Although you are in control of the movements of the machine, the width of the zigzag still has to be set. However, the spacing of the stitch depends on the speed at which the frame is moved (fig. 61).

28

Fig. 62 Free machine embroidery on unbleached calico can produce a variety of textures. (Janet Cave)

Fig. 63

Fig. 64

Fig. 65

Fig. 66

Fig. 67

Fig. 68

Fig. 69

Circular movements are also possible with the zigzag (fig. 63), but it is not possible to make the stitches radiate from a circle simply by using circular movements of the ring. It is necessary to work them in small sections, stopping and turning the ring for each section (fig. 64).

A more raised line can be produced by loosening the bottom tension slightly and tightening the top one again slightly, so that the top thread sits on the surface of the fabric and the bottom one comes up and just binds over it, couching it down (fig. 65). In order to achieve the best effects with this, it is necessary to move the work very slowly so that the top thread is more or less hidden by the bottom one.

A more exaggerated version of this can also be produced by loosening the bottom tension a great deal more and tightening the top one a little. The bottom thread should now stand up in fairly large loops (fig. 66). Circular movements using this technique give a particularly attractive effect (fig. 67).

It is also possible to obtain a heavier texture by putting a thicker thread in the bottom. This is usually something which you cannot use on the top of the machine, such as fine wool, cotton perlé or floss silk. The bottom tension will need to be loosened in order to accommodate the additional thickness of thread, and the top tension will also require some adjustment as it should couch the bottom thread on the underside (fig. 68). Remember to reverse the fabric before you use this technique as it has to be worked from the wrong side of the fabric.

Another, much rougher texture can be produced by removing the tension screw from the bobbin case, so that there is no bottom tension (fig. 69). Keep a thick thread on the bobbin and set a similar top tension to the last technique. This produces a much more knobbly texture.

Cut work done on the machine can produce some very delicate effects and could be useful in certain types of Church embroidery, particularly for altar linen. It is best to use cotton organdie for experiments with this technique although cut work can be done on other fabrics once the technique is mastered. Use a normal tension, as for dressmaking, when working. First of all, machine a line of straight stitching around the shape which is to be cut out (fig. 70). Take a small pair of sharp, pointed scissors and cut out the shape just inside the line of stitching, cutting very close to it, but taking care not to cut the threads. Then put the machine needle into the fabric just outside the line of stitching and proceed to machine across the hole, anchoring the cord produced at the other side just outside the stitching line (fig. 71). Throw a series of these cords across the hole in various directions until there is a reasonable network of threads. It should now be possible to work into these threads in order to produce broader bands or shapes within the hole. This is done simply by machining backwards and forwards across a group of threads, starting from the middle and working towards the outside (fig. 72). The stitching should be fairly close together. The cords can also be brought together into a series of groups by machining in a circular fashion around various intersections (fig. 73).

When the middle is complete, neaten the outside edge with a satin stitch. For this set the machine on a fairly wide zigzag stitch, and work the stitch in very small sections, turning the work after each section in order to make the stitches radiate from the centre (fig. 74).

Some beautiful effects can be achieved with cut work, but you need to practise quite a lot to achieve a good standard of technique.

Canvas stitches

There is not much scope for canvas embroidery in the ecclesiastical field and it is usually restricted to kneelers, although it is also possible to use it for such furnishings as altar carpets. Its most important characteristic is that it is very practical and hard wearing and this should always be borne in mind. It does not mean that the result will necessarily be dull; in fact very rich effects can be obtained from canvas stitches. It is a great pity that so few people experiment with them because the stitches themselves are exciting and give surface pattern and texture to the work which cannot be obtained in any other way (fig. 75). Unfortunately, the vast majority of embroiderers are familiar with only three canvas stitches at the most – tent stitch, cross stitch and Florentine stitch – and do not even combine these in the same piece of work; consequently, the result is rather dreary.

When working on canvas, there are one or two points to remember. Perhaps the most important one and something

Fig. 70

Fig. 71

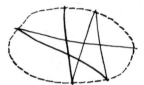

Fig. 72

Fig. 73

Fig. 74

Fig. 75 Canvas stitches which show some interesting surface textures. (Jill Woolley)

which may be rather obvious is that the stitches work over counted thread. It is essential to count the threads correctly because if a mistake is made it becomes very obvious as the work progresses, rather like a dropped stitch in knitting.

Another point of fundamental importance is to choose wool thick enough to cover the canvas properly. The canvas should not show when the work is finished. If it does, the article will not wear very well; it can be compared to a carpet with a thin pile. The thickness of the wool depends mainly on the size of the mesh of the canvas. If a fine canvas is used, obviously a finer wool will be required. Sometimes the structure of the stitch itself also affects the coverage. Stitches worked on the straight of the canvas do not usually cover it so well as those worked on the diagonal. There are various methods of overcoming this, but some change the appearance of the stitch; the simplest method therefore is sometimes to use a thicker thread.

There are two types of canvas; one with a single mesh and the other with a double mesh (fig. 76). The single mesh is more versatile and easier to work on, particularly for beginners. Canvas is made in cotton and linen; linen is the more durable and also the more expensive. A cotton canvas is, however, useful for samples. It comes in a variety of sizes which are determined by the number of threads per inch. Sixteen or eighteen threads to the inch are both fairly reasonable sizes for working small pieces of canvas work, although if the canvas is for a carpet a rug mesh might be more suitable, depending on the size and design of the finished article.

Two kinds of thread are manufactured for canvas work. The most popular is tapestry wool, the other is crewel wool which is much finer. These may be supplemented by other threads to give additional interest to the work. Knitting yarns are useful and sometimes cheaper if large quantities of the same colour are required. Rug yarns are also obtainable but the range of colours is rather limited. Thrums, which are short lengths of yarn remaining when a carpet is cut from the loom, can be used. The lengths are usually quite suitable for working and it is possible to obtain a much wider colour range than is available in rug yarn. Both rug yarn and thrums are more suitable for carpets but they can also be used for kneelers. The result, however, tends to be rather coarse.

Basically, there are two types of canvas stitch; one is based on the diagonal, and the other on the straight of the mesh threads. Some of the stitches, such as shell stitch (fig. 77) and rococo stitch (fig. 78), are decorative in themselves and do not therefore require an elaborate design. Many of the simpler stitches can be made extremely decorative just by changing the colour or tone of the threads in each row or block of stitches; this can be done with Florentine stitch, Hungarian stitch (fig. 79), and Scotch stitch (fig. 80), to name but a few.

32

Fig. 76

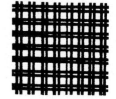

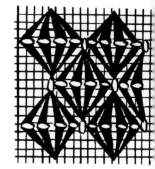

Fig. 77

Fig. 78

Fig. 79

Fig. 80

Fig. 81   Red altar frontal
representing the crown of glory,
designed for Christ Church
Cathedral, Hamilton, Ontario,
Canada. (Dorothy Gregson)

Fig. 82 Detail of embroidery
using felt, gold kid, acetate, silk,
cords and metal threads.
(Jill Woolley)

While it is not always desirable to use a large number of different stitches when working a piece of embroidery, it is a good idea to try out several stitches beforehand, and experiment with them by changing the scale and colour to see what effects can be obtained. Experiments of this kind can help tremendously when designing the finished article.

There are two ways in which to start stitching on canvas. One method is to weave the thread in and out of the mesh for about eight or nine threads, and then stitch over it so that it is completely covered. The other method is to knot the end of the thread and put the needle through the canvas from right to wrong side, a few inches away from where stitching is to start. As the canvas is covered the thread will be secured at the back of the work and the knot can be cut off. To finish a length of thread darn it into the back of the area of stitching as neatly as possible. After the first block of stitchery darn the new threads into the existing areas of embroidery.

When experimenting with stitches, it is advisable to work them in a series of blocks which touch each other. This helps you to see some of the problems created by using a variety of stitches in canvas work. The main stumbling block is fitting the stitches together satisfactorily so that no threads of canvas can be seen between them. If the stitches are tried out next to each other, such problems can be resolved before you embark on the finished work and you will be aware of them when designing.

Some stitches do not give adequate coverage of the canvas because of their structure. One method of overcoming this is to use tramming. This is a long stitch of the same thread taken across the row occupied by that particular stitch. The stitch is then worked over the thread, at right angles to it (fig. 83). This method is not suitable for all stitches and other stitches can be dealt with by inserting small back stitches to fill in the gaps. These must be done regularly, of course, otherwise they will ruin the appearance of the work. They will, of course, change the appearance of the stitch.

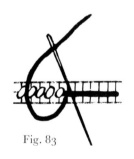

Fig. 83

Metal threads

Many people consider gold work synonymous with ecclesiastical embroidery, but few are fully aware of the variety of threads available or their possibilities. There are a number of threads specially manufactured for this purpose in gold and silver. They are not obtainable in all shops selling embroidery materials, but can be purchased from certain specialists. Perhaps the most common of these threads is Japanese gold. This is manufactured from gold leaf, mounted on tissue paper which is cut into thin strips and twisted around a core of orange silk. It is sold in a skein and comes in various sizes, 1K being the thickest.

There are also a number of cords made from twisted Japanese gold threads. These provide an even thicker thread. At the

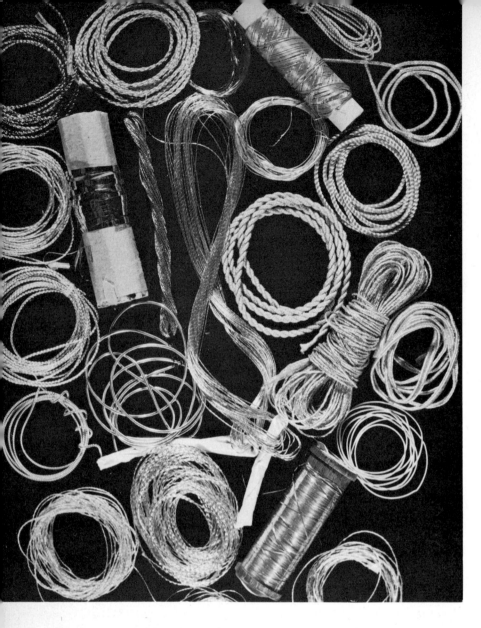

Fig. 84 Some of the many metal threads which can be used for gold work.

other end of the scale there are some very fine threads known as tambour and passing threads.

The other gold and silver threads available are not strictly threads at all and are not really used as such. The first is plate. This is a fine, flat strip of metal approximately $\frac{1}{10}$ inch (2.5 mm) wide. Then there are the purls; these are made from thin wire twisted to give various surface finishes and to look like a thread. Each finish comes in a number of thicknesses. Pearl purl or bead purl is a rather stiff wire with a very obvious coil. Rough, smooth and check purl are all rather soft and pliable. Rough purl has a comparatively dull surface, smooth purl is very bright and shiny and check purl has a sparkling, chequered surface. All these threads are obtainable in both pure gold and

36

silver. The silver, unfortunately, has a strong tendency to tarnish in a short period of time.

Today gold and silver threads are usually supplemented with other metal threads in order to provide additional interest and to cut down the cost. There are many threads which are suitable for this. All of the Lurex yarns can be used and there are a number of aluminium threads available which are an improvement on silver as they do not tarnish. There is also quite a variety of metallic-coloured cords and braids available which are also very useful.

An imitation Japanese gold thread can also be bought. It is useful for practice but does not have the same quality as the real Japanese gold thread. Its characteristics when working are totally different. It can, of course, also be used on finished work.

Gold and silver threads are very expensive and can easily be damaged; take great care when storing them. Japanese gold thread is supplied in a skein but it is unwise to leave it like this for very long as the thread easily becomes twisted and bent, revealing the core of orange silk. Although you twist the thread when working, it is not always possible to correct previous damage and consequently a whole area may have to be wasted. Make a roll of felt and wind the thread onto it. The felt should be tightly coiled until it reaches about 1 inch (25 mm) in diameter, and it should be approximately $4\frac{1}{2}$–5 inches (11–12.5 cm) long. Sew down the end firmly so that the roll does not become slack. Wind the Japanese gold carefully onto the roll; and it will then be ready for use. When not in use it should be wrapped in tissue paper.

Smooth, rough, and check purl are even more easily damaged. They should be carefully wrapped in tissue paper when not in use. Take care not to stretch or squash them.

When working with metal threads you must stretch the fabric in a frame. Normally a square frame is used but for small experiments an embroidery ring is reasonably satisfactory.

The techniques used for metal threads are somewhat different from other types of embroidery. The threads are not pulled through the fabric except at the beginning and end of a row or section because they are so easily damaged. Effects are gained almost entirely from various forms of couching. Threads are couched singly or in pairs and a wide variety of effects can be obtained if the technique is properly exploited. First experiments are easier if worked in a single thread as the thread has to be twisted with the left hand while you sew with the right, in order to prevent the orange silk from showing between the strips of gold. This does not, however, apply to imitation Japanese gold.

When couching metal threads, it is usual to leave both ends of the thread on the surface of the work until they get in the way or until there are several to finish off together (fig. 85); otherwise you are constantly turning the work over, which

Fig. 85

37

can be a nuisance with a large frame and slows up the rate of working. The threads are usually couched with Maltese silk, sometimes known as horsetail. This is manufactured in two shades of gold and silver grey. However, it is possible to use other coloured threads to obtain different effects. The couching thread is usually waxed first in order to prevent tangles and knots and also to strengthen it. This is done by drawing the thread across a piece of beeswax.

The placing of the stitches is of great importance because, even with an apparently matching thread, in certain lights the stitches are clearly visible and any slight variation is immediately obvious. It is possible to vary the tone of the gold by using different coloured couching threads. If you use a blue thread the gold appears colder; if you use red the gold has a warm appearance.

Various surface patterns can be achieved by the positioning of the couching stitches (fig. 86). Couching stitches are usually single and evenly spaced, but they can be grouped or unevenly spaced to give particular effects. However, if this is done, the effect should look intentional rather than the result of plain bad technique. It is obvious when it is the latter.

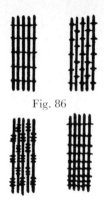

Fig. 86

Fig. 87 Experimental sample of gold work using padded kid, a variety of metal threads, mirrorflex and beads.
(Cheryl Welsh)

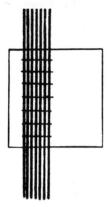

Fig. 88

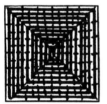

Fig. 89

Fig. 90

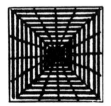

Fig. 91

If a shape is to be filled with couching, give careful consideration to the direction of the thread. Metal threads are shiny and therefore catch the light a great deal with even the slightest movement; consequently the direction of metal threads plays a particularly important part in the design. Threads can be taken across a shape in one direction only, and a new piece of thread is used for each line (fig. 88). A totally different effect can be obtained by couching a continuous thread to fill a shape, starting with the outside (fig. 89). This creates a number of facets which will catch the light. If you want an even texture omit stitches at regular intervals as you approach the centre of the shape (fig. 90). You can obtain a shaded effect by retaining the stitches. The central area will become very heavily stitched (fig. 91), almost obliterating the metal thread. Similar effects can be obtained when couching a circle. If you couch a shape in this manner, begin stitching around the outside of the shape, working towards the middle. This will ensure that you produce a better shape than you would produce by starting to stitch in the middle and working outwards.

You can obtain raised textures with an area of couching by sewing down pieces of string at right angles to the direction of the couching and then proceeding to couch over the top of it (fig. 92). The string should be smooth, strong and tightly twisted so that it has a relatively even surface. It can be dyed yellow so that it does not show when gold thread is couched over it. If the string is sufficiently close together you can build up various patterns, both formal and informal (fig. 93). The string itself can also be couched in a much more informal manner and if the metal threads are couched equally informally over the top, some very interesting textures can result (fig. 94). Different thicknesses of string can also add subtle variations.

Another method of producing raised shapes with an area of couching is to cut shapes of felt or card and sew them down within the area to be couched and then proceed to couch over them without catching the metal thread down over the area of the felt or paper shape underneath (fig. 95). This results in relatively smooth areas within the couched shape, which have a greater tendency to catch the light.

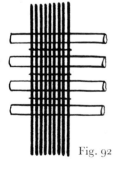

Fig. 92

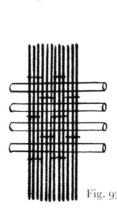

Fig. 93

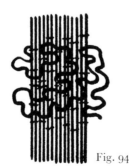

Fig. 94

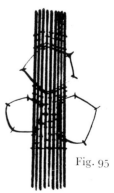

Fig. 95

Turning corners can be a problem, particularly when using Japanese gold and silver thread. The more acute the angle, the more difficult it becomes. Perhaps the most obvious method is to place a stitch where the thread is turned, bringing the needle up on the inside and taking the thread across to the outside of the angle (fig. 96). If the angle is very acute (fig. 97), the Japanese gold thread must be twisted much more tightly at this point to avoid the orange silk showing between the strips of gold.

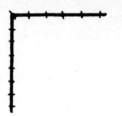

Fig. 96

When you couch a double thread the problem becomes slightly more complicated. Starting at one of the angles, catch the single thread in the middle by a small stitch, and then fold it to form a double thread (fig. 98). Take a single couching stitch across both the threads. If the angle is fairly acute, continue with the outside thread and cut the inside one, slotting in another thread a short distance below the finished one (fig. 99). This creates a much neater angle than continuous threads do.

Fig. 97

The method used for finishing off the ends of Japanese gold and silver thread differs somewhat from that used in other types of embroidery. The thread is not taken directly through the fabric with a needle. Thread a tapestry or chenille needle with a strong thread, such as soft embroidery cotton, and bring the needle up through the fabric at the finishing point for the metal thread. Then take the needle back through the fabric in exactly the same hole that it entered, leaving a loop. Push the metal thread through this loop. Hold the two ends of the soft embroidery cotton quite firmly and give them a gentle tug. This should pull the metal thread through the fabric onto the wrong side without damaging it. If you are using a thick thread or cord, you can make a hole in the material with a stiletto before you make the soft embroidery cotton loop. Keep the end of the metal thread in position on the wrong side of the work by oversewing. Because of the structure of metal threads, it will still be possible for it to come through to the right side again if it gets caught in something and therefore, as well as oversewing it, you should fray out the ends of the thread to create a greater mass which should keep it in position. This method is sometimes also useful for finishing other types of thick thread when they are too big to go through the eye of a needle.

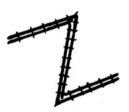

Fig. 98

Fig. 99

Gold and silver plate is not usually taken through the fabric. To start working bend the plate over and hold the piece that is bent with a few stitches. These will not be visible from the top. The plate can then be couched like an ordinary thread. Finish it off as you started.

In addition to ordinary couching, plate has other possibilities because of its structure. When you bend it, plate can retain the bend. So you can produce decorative effects by pressing it over various surfaces. One of the most interesting is to hold the plate

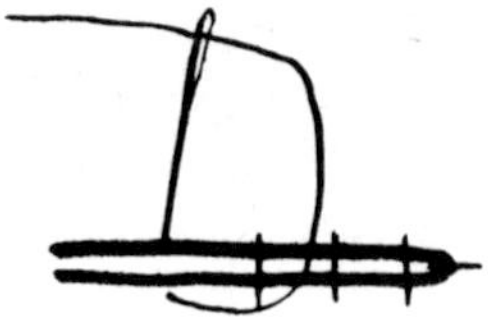

Fig. 100

Fig. 101

lengthwise down the thread of a screw and press it into the indentations of the thread with the thumb nail (fig. 100). This results in a permanent crimped effect; the plate can then be couched. Similar effects can be gained by holding it along the teeth of a comb, and a number of other uneven surfaces could be used for experiments.

There is a way of sewing plate down over an area without any stitches being visible. Begin at one end of a shape in the normal way and bring the plate across the shape on a slight diagonal. Catch it down with a stitch and then fold the plate back in the other direction, again on a slight diagonal, and stitch it down on the other side (fig. 101), continuing until the shape is filled. Finish in the usual manner. The shape should be completely filled by a line of zigzag plate with no stitches visible. Strips of plate can be woven together before you fix them onto the fabric.

Purls are not treated in the same way as threads. They are not taken through the fabric at all and should therefore be cut to the required length before you start working. Purls are similar to fine wire and are usually cut with a small, tough pair

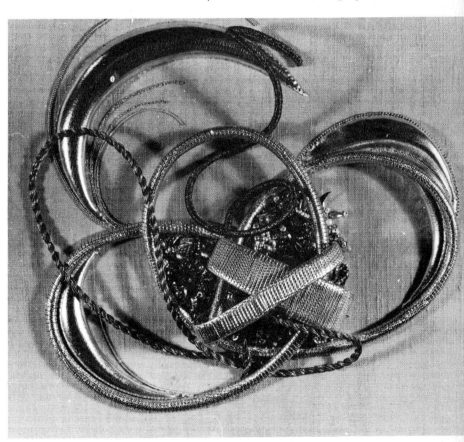

Fig. 102 · Experimental sample using gold threads over tubing, cane and plastic spirals, and padded plastic kid. The centre is heavily encrusted with a variety of beads and sequins.
(Brenda Marchbank)

Fig. 103 Detail of embroidery
using metal threads, padded kid,
purls and net. (Sheila Toone)

of scissors; nail scissors with straight blades are quite satisfactory. Keep the scissors at right angles to the purl when cutting, otherwise the ends of the purl will become bent. It is advisable to cut purl on a piece of felt as it rolls easily and often the pieces are so small they are difficult to find. It is also easier to pick them up from felt. If you have planned a great deal of work with purl, the felt can be stuck onto a piece of card of a convenient size, which you can move around while you work.

Pearl purl has somewhat different possibilities to the other purls because of its stiffness. Unlike the others it can be couched, and by pulling the thread a little you can force it between the coils to make it invisible. It also looks rather attractive if you pull the end so that the coil opens up and then couch it as a thread. The ends of the pearl purl should be firmly sewn down; otherwise they will catch in things. This type of purl can also be cut in short lengths, resembling beads, and sewn down like beads with a beading needle.

Rough, smooth and check purl cannot be couched as they are too soft, so treat them like beads. Cut the purl to the

Fig. 104

Fig. 105

Fig. 106

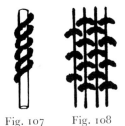

Fig. 107   Fig. 108

Fig. 109

required lengths and sew down like beads, using a beading needle. Even within the technical limitations you can produce quite a variety of textures. Purls are manufactured in several thicknesses and if you cut these into varying lengths it adds interest to the work. They can be sewn down in a scattered way to produce an open texture (fig. 104) or very close together to produce a much thicker, heavier one (fig. 105). The textures can be free or more formal, producing small geometric patterns (fig. 106).

Another asset of these purls is their pliability. This can be used to great effect and can add another dimension to your work. If a length of string or some gold cord is sewn down onto the background fabric, short lengths of purl can be sewn across it. This can be done at right angles, but it looks much more effective if it is done in a sloping line (fig. 107). If you use a variety of purls, both in texture and thickness, you can create even more subtle effects. Instead of using string or cord as a base, you can sew purls over each other. The string or cord can be substituted by a length of purl and you can sew shorter lengths across the top (fig. 108). In this way, small areas of texture or pattern can be built up, formally or informally. It is possible to make the purls stand away from the surface of the fabric in loops without any support underneath by cutting a longer length of purl than is required and stitching it down with a short stitch as if it were a small bead. Because it is pliable the purl forms a loop and stands up from the background fabric (fig. 109).

Before you start work on a piece of ecclesiastical embroidery it is useful to experiment with these techniques involved in using metal threads. You will not only become familiar with them, but will also discover for yourself their aesthetic possibilities. The techniques described above are only a guide; many variations can be evolved from them and these in turn can be given even more variety by the combination of various types of metal thread. Don't just try out the various techniques but try fitting them together into a small composition to see how they relate to each other. At this stage it is best not to be too concerned with ecclesiastical design, as that involves other problems, but to enjoy experimenting with the threads.

3 Furnishings and Vestments Suitable for Embroidery

Not all vestments and furnishings are particularly suited to embroidery. Often you can obtain much more effective results by confining embroidery to a few related furnishings and vestments, rather than embellishing every piece of fabric that is visible in the church. Indeed, a beautiful piece of plain fabric can greatly enhance a nearby piece of embroidery.

With the liturgical movement a new visual emphasis has been placed on the altar and the priest's vestments. When the altar is placed in a more central position in a church, it can be seen more easily by the congregation and therefore takes on a

Fig. 110 Laudian altar frontal designed for St Mungo's Cathedral, Glasgow, Scotland. (Malcolm Lochhead)

Fig. 111 Opposite side of the
altar frontal designed for
St Mungo's. The background is
a patchwork of various colours of
Sekers silk and the central
decoration, a padded structure
covered with kid, is removable.
(Malcolm Lochhead)

new visual significance. Often it is free-standing, which means
that it can be viewed from all sides and does not have a screen
immediately behind it. In this situation the old type of altar
frontal is no longer useful, as it was designed to be viewed
from the front only. The Laudian or throw-over frontal is
probably the best method of dealing with this situation, as it
can have decoration on all sides.

As the priest now faces the congregation in the new order of
service, instead of conducting much of the service with his back
to them, the front of the chasuble has become as important as
the back, and also requires some decoration.

By no means all churches have adopted the new order of
service and not all priests have the new garments, so it is
necessary to give details of furnishings and vestments, and leave
it up to the individual to select what is required by a particular
church.

A wide variety of techniques can be incorporated in the vestments and furnishings although there are, of course, limitations
of practicality and scale.

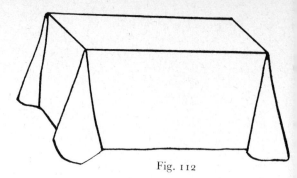

Fig. 112

Furnishings

The altar frontal

Basically there are two types of frontal. The simplest in form is the Laudian or throw-over one, which resembles a huge table-cloth in an exotic fabric and is thrown over the altar to touch the ground on all sides (fig. 112). This type of frontal is usually used if the altar is free-standing, and has become popular with the introduction of the new order of service in the Church of England. The dimensions of a Laudian altar frontal depend upon the height, length and depth of the altar. As there is no standard size for altars, you must take careful measurements to work out the dimensions of the frontal.

The more familiar type of frontal is the one which is used on the front of the altar (fig. 113). It is usual for the altar to be at the east end of the church, more or less against the wall or with a screen immediately behind it. In these circumstances a Laudian frontal is unnecessary.

There are several variations of the ordinary frontal, depending on the method of attaching it. Modern altar frontals do not usually have a super-frontal or frontlet – a thin strip of fabric, either plain or embroidered, the width of the altar frontal and approximately 3–6 inches (7.5–15 cm) deep. Consequently, the frontal must finish flush with the top edge of the altar. Its dimensions would be the height multiplied by the length of the altar, plus seam allowances. There are several possible ways of attaching the frontal to the altar, although it is usually attached to a piece of linen which goes over the top of the altar.

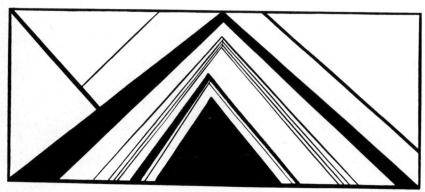

Fig. 113

Fig. 114 White altar frontal for
St James's Anglican Church,
Dundas, Ontario, Canada. The
background is moiré with applied
shapes in various other fabrics.
(Margaret Wallace)

1 The top of the frontal is attached to a piece of linen which
is long enough to go over the top of the altar and hang down
at the back. The unattached end of the linen has a hem of
approximately 2 inches (5 cm) which is open at both ends. A
metal rod is inserted in the hem and its weight keeps the frontal
in position (fig. 115). If so desired, a continuous piece of linen
can be used behind the frontal as well to replace the normal
lining.

47

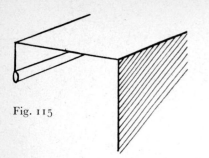

Fig. 115

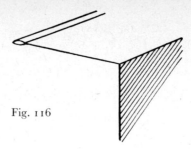

Fig. 116

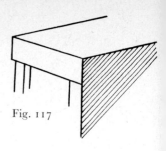

Fig. 117

2   The method described above can be adapted to fit an altar which is flush with the wall or reredos by shortening the linen and placing a flat rod in the hem at the back of the top of the altar (fig. 116).

3   A fitted linen cover can be made for the top and sides of the altar. The depth of the sides and back should be about 7–8 inches (18–20 cm) when finished. The frontal is then stitched to the front edge (fig. 117).

4   The embroidery can be stretched over a wooden frame which has been constructed to fit underneath the altar or to be fixed to the front. Usually the frame is covered with un-bleached calico first of all and the embroidery is stretched over it. Drawing pins are used to hold it in position during the preliminary stages; they can later be replaced by small nails (fig. 118). While this method of making up can give a very smooth appearance to the work, remember that it can cause storage problems, as it is not usual to take the frontal off the frame once it has been stretched.

5   This method involves the use of hooks on the altar over which the frontal is placed. A series of tabs made from linen are attached to the frontal and a metal rod is slotted through them (fig. 119). The rod is then placed over the hooks on the altar and this is covered by a super-frontal, which is fixed in the same way as methods 1, 2 or 3.

6   A method similar to 5 can be used without a super-frontal but the position of the hooks may have to be raised and the linen tabs attached to the back of the frontal a few inches below the top, so that the rod and hooks are not visible (fig. 120).

If you use methods 5 or 6 the frontals do not need to be quite so deep as those using the earlier methods. Have a good look at the altar before you start work on the frontal.

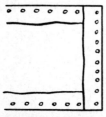

Fig. 118

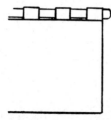

Fig. 119

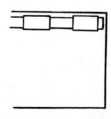

Fig. 120

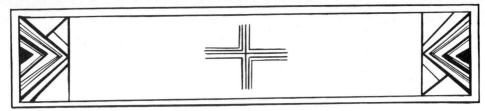

Fig. 121

The fair linen or altar-cloth

The cloth is always of white linen, but you can use a coarser linen with a slub instead of the traditional fine linen. It must cover the top of the altar and usually hangs down over the sides (fig. 121). Because of the variation in altar shapes there are no standard measurements and therefore each individual altar must be measured before you start any embroidery for it. The finished cloth should measure the exact width of the top of the altar.

The embroidery is usually in white but need not be traditional in technique. There is plenty of scope for machine embroidery as well as hand embroidery, although this approach seldom seems to be used. However, do not forget that the cloth is laundeerd frequently, as a tablecloth would be, and the embroidery must be strong enough to withstand this.

The burse

The burse or corporal case resembles a book with no pages (fig. 122), in which the corporal is kept when not in use. It is approximately 9 inches (23 cm) square and is hinged at one side. The top of the design is at the hinged side because the burse usually stands hinge-side uppermost when it is placed over the chalice veil upon the chalice. It can be very richly embroidered and should match the vestments of the day, bearing in mind the rules concerning liturgical colours.

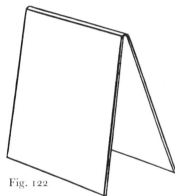

Fig. 122

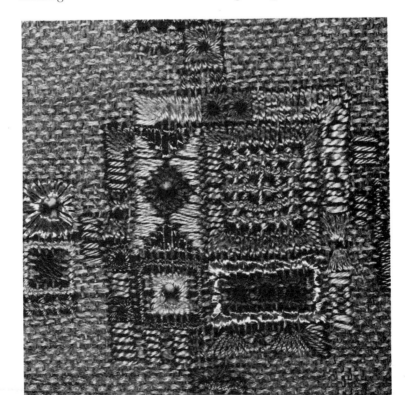

Fig. 123 Detail of pulled work cross on uneven-weave fabric, suitable for an altar-cloth. Various threads have been used, including cotton perlé, raffine, crochet cotton, acrylic thread, coton à broder and stranded cotton. (Brenda Marchbank)

The dossal

The dossal is the hanging behind the altar which is either like a curtain or flat and mounted on a stretcher (fig. 125). The size varies according to the fittings available and the style of dossal required; take careful measurements of the fittings before designing the embroidery. The dossal offers a designer much more scope in a modern church where, in certain circumstances, it is possible to make it much larger than the conventional type, and so give a much greater emphasis to the altar. This can become a magnificent focal point in an otherwise plain church.

Fig. 124 Cream-coloured burse embroidered with a variety of metal threads and purls, gold kid, coloured acetate and sequins. (Pat Beese)

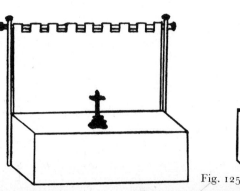

Fig. 125

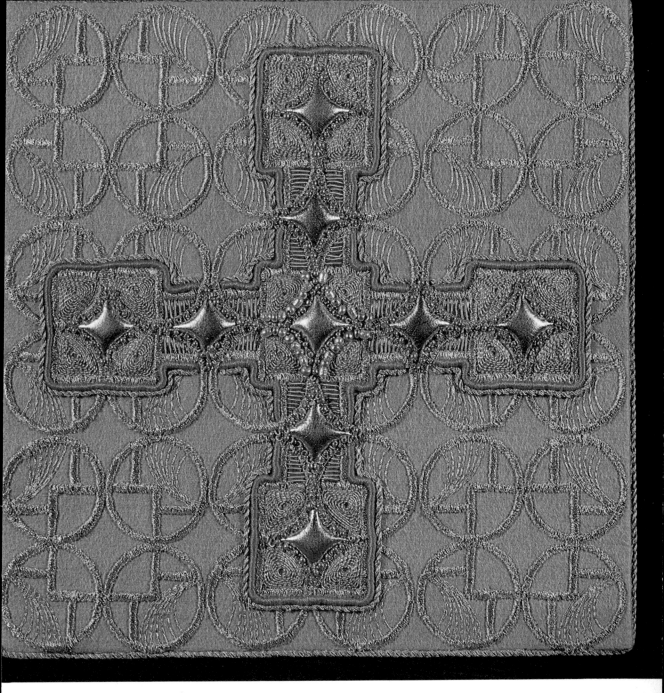

Fig. 126 Burse with schiffli
embroidery as a base, enriched
with padded silver kid, cords,
beads and purls. (Gail Kemp)

52

Fig. 127 Red chasuble designed for Loughborough Parish Church, England. Padded silver kid, blue leather and suède, yellow braid and metal threads were used for the embroidery. (Pat Collins)

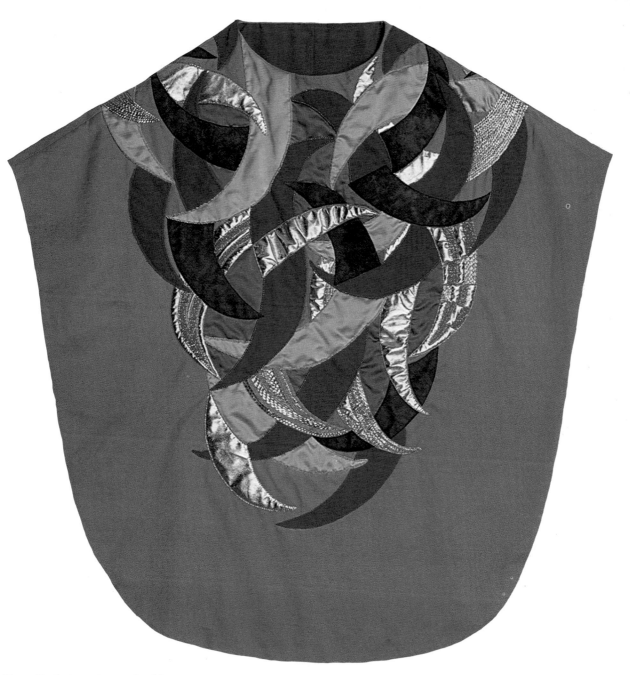

Fig. 128 Satin, velvet and gold
kid shapes have been enriched
with metal threads on this
chasuble designed for
Loughborough Parish Church,
England. It is lined with red silk.
(Gwen Carey)

53

Fig. 129 Chasuble designed for
Loughborough Parish Church,
England. Padded gold kid, suède,
velvet pile fabric, raw silk,
chenille and metal threads were
used.
(Ann Greenwood)

Banners vary considerably in size according to their purpose. However, one thing is important – that it should be possible to carry them reasonably easily.

If you are planning a completely new banner, decide upon the pole and fittings before you start to design because these will affect the dimensions. When you have taken careful measurements you can work out the size and shape. Banners need not be square or rectangular in shape; in fact they offer

Fig. 130 Restricted colour on a grey background has been used for this hanging. The dark stripes are applied strips of hand weaving and the remaining shapes are applied and enriched with machine embroidery. (Anne Hunter)

Fig. 131   A banner using a
variety of fabrics with simple
shapes applied by machine.
(Margaret Wallace)

quite a lot of scope for variation (fig. 132), and it is worth
experimenting a little before you make a definite decision.

The design also needs a great deal of thought. If the banner
is to remain in the church as a permanent fixture, then it is
important that it fits in with the general scheme of things. A
banner which clashes permanently with everything in sight is
not a pleasant thing to look at! So give very careful consideration to colour and design generally. There is no reason why
the design should not be bold in treatment, using large areas
of appliqué, for example, to obtain the major shapes.

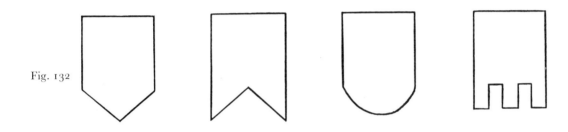

Fig. 132

The pulpit fall

The pulpit fall can make a useful focal point in a church
because of its position. Its size is variable and depends on the
size of the stand. The hanging section is usually longer than
the width to make a more pleasing proportion (fig. 133).
However, in order to determine the size, individual measurements should be taken and various proportions tried out.

The embroidery can be very rich here. Most churches
prefer to follow the liturgical colours and the embroidery
should therefore be designed accordingly. However, it is not
absolutely necessary to follow tradition on this point.

Pulpit falls have a particular importance in Free Churches
and are often the only piece of embroidery in the church.
Therefore in some ways perhaps they offer more scope than
those for the Anglican Church.

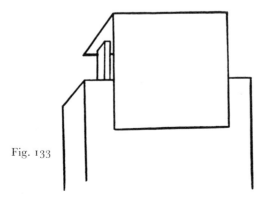

Fig. 133

Fig. 134 Pulpit fall representing the Holy Spirit breaking through Church buildings. The background is orange-pink with applied fabrics and kid. The centre is padded and the whole enriched with metal threads. (Kathleen Whyte)

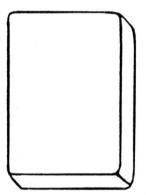

Fig. 135

Kneelers

The average size for a kneeler (fig. 135) is approximately 9 × 12 × 3 inches (23 × 30 × 7.5 cm). Hassocks can be deeper and a little larger. They are usually made of embroidered canvas or canvas work, as it is better known, in order to make them sufficiently hardwearing. Other types of embroidery could be used, but they would have to be very practical indeed as well as being smooth enough for comfort. There are, however, possibilities of using leather or suède in this context.

Basically there are two methods of making up a modern kneeler and both of these affect the design somewhat. You must decide which method you are going to use before you start work. The first method involves making the top and sides in one piece (fig. 136). With the second method, the sides are embroidered separately and joined to the top later (fig. 137). The latter method obviously requires more canvas as, although the pieces may be worked close together, sufficient canvas must be left for turnings.

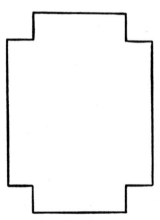

Fig. 136

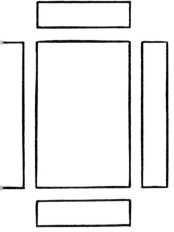

Fig. 137

Figs 138 and 139   Kneelers
designed to go with the Laudian
altar frontal in St Mungo's
Cathedral, Glasgow, Scotland
(figs 110 and 111). They
demonstrate various canvas
techniques and are worked in
tapisserie wools and gold and
silver fingering.
(Malcom Lochhead)

Carpets

Altar carpets present a problem in many churches. Usually they tend to be of an antique Persian variety and, whilst very beautiful in themselves, they are often totally unsuited to the other furnishings in the church. Embroidered carpets are not widely used but could be an ideal subject for a group project. Basically, the techniques are similar to those used in canvas work for kneelers but on a much larger scale. Because of its size, a carpet offers great scope for design and technique and if well thought out could make a tremendous visual impact.

Again there are no average sizes which can be quoted, as church interiors vary considerably, but if properly measured your carpet could be fitted much more accurately than a Persian one made to a standard size.

Vestments

The cope

The cope is basically a semicircular cloak (fig. 140) which is worn for ceremonial purposes by archbishops, bishops, deacons and subdeacons. It is usually made of a rich fabric and can be lavishly embroidered.

If it is worn by the celebrant it is customary to conform to the liturgical colour, but otherwise it can be a colour in keeping with the general furnishings and vestments.

Occasionally the shoulders of the cope are shaped by appropriate seams but the semicircular cope is much simpler. A band or border usually called an orphrey can be used along the straight edge; this can be embroidered if you like. Medieval copes were embroidered with an all-over pattern and a border; in some ways this is more interesting, if treated in an up-to-date manner, than merely placing an embroidered motif on the back.

At one time the cope had a hood attached at the back of the neck. Most traditional copes have a vestige of it which is now purely decorative. This, however, is not particularly fashionable for modern copes and the design is much more effective without it.

The neck edge of the cope can be slightly shaped if you think it should lie flatter.

The cope is fastened at the front either by fabric tabs, which are held in position by hooks and eyes, or a metal clasp. This fastening is known as a morse.

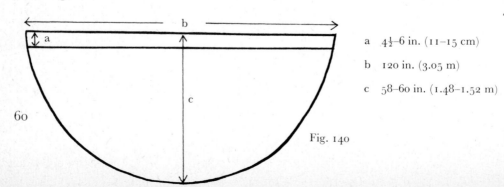

a   4½–6 in. (11–15 cm)

b   120 in. (3.05 m)

c   58–60 in. (1.48–1.52 m)

60

Fig. 140

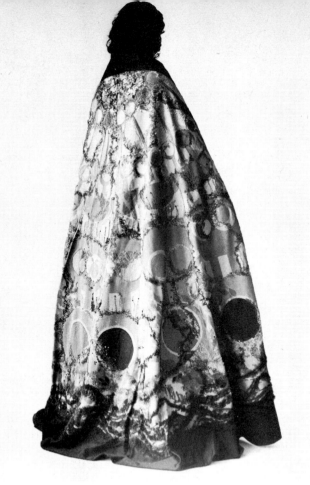

Fig. 141 Cope in various shades of green and gold on a green background. Some of the shapes have been printed, others are applied and the whole has been enriched with machine embroidery. (Lyn Nicol)

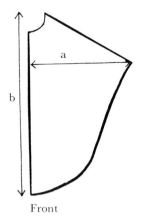

Front

a Approx. 25 in. (64 cm)

b Approx. 46 in. (1.17 m)

Back

Fig. 142

The chasuble

The chasuble resembles a poncho in shape, although it is much longer, and is worn in the same way. It is more or less the key garment of the vestments because they are usually made in sets with the design and colour relating to those of the chasuble. Chasubles offer a great deal of scope for design and are made in a rich fabric.

The shape can vary quite a bit, although there are basically three main shapes. They are, namely, the Gothic chasuble (fig. 142), the conical (fig. 143), and the Gothic revival (fig. 144). Of these, the Gothic one is most popular today.

Traditionally the embroidery was placed on the back, but it is now usual to embroider both back and front.

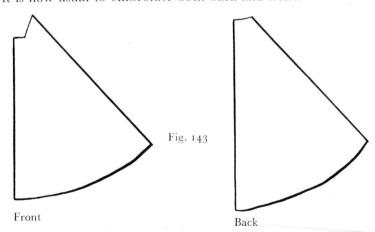

Front

Fig. 143

Back

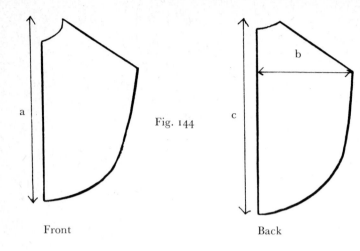

a   Approx. 50 in. (1.27 m)

b   Approx. 25 in. (64 cm)

c   Approx. 54 in. (1.37 m)

Fig. 144

Front   Back

Fig. 145   Chasuble in blue wool based on the Alpha and Omega theme. The symbols are applied and enriched with hand stitchery. (Jean Stanhope)

62

The stole

This is totally unlike the article of the same name worn by women. It is very long and thin, being only about 3½ inches (9 cm) at its widest point, although it can be a little wider if it is worn without a chasuble (fig. 147). Basically, there are two types of stole. One is worn with the chasuble and the other without. If it is worn with the chasuble it must be considerably longer than the other type which just hangs around the neck and falls to about 12–18 inches (30–46 cm) from the ground. When it is worn under the chasuble it is crossed over and held at the waist with a girdle. This naturally takes up a much greater length. The ends of the stole usually project below the chasuble for approximately 12 inches (30 cm) and the stole is therefore only embroidered for about that distance at each end. It also has a tiny cross or motif at the back of the neck, over the seam. The stole is cut from two pieces of fabric along the straight of the fabric and the neck is shaped by a diagonal seam.

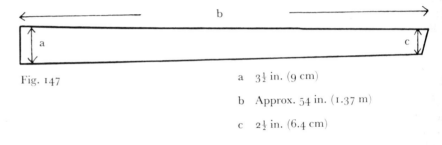

Fig. 147

a 3½ in. (9 cm)

b Approx. 54 in. (1.37 m)

c 2½ in. (6.4 cm)

The amice and the apparel

The amice is made from a rectangle of white linen approximately 36 × 24 inches (91 × 61 cm), with tapes at one end. Attached to this is a long narrow strip of embroidery approximately 20 × 3 inches (51 × 7.5 cm) when finished (fig. 148). The embroidered apparel, as it is known, is usually made from the same fabric as the vestments and corresponds with them. There is one apparel for each set. It can be richly embroidered and is fixed to the amice by any detachable method, so that the amice can be laundered. The whole article is put on over the priest's head and forms a kind of neck-cloth or collar.

Recently, a new garment has been designed which renders the amice and apparel unnecessary but few clergy possess it and sets of vestments will need an apparel until such time as the under-garments are replaced.

Fig. 146   Detail of embroidery on a stole (fig. 213). (Pat Beese)

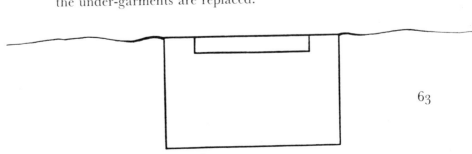

Fig. 148

63

4 Liturgical Colours

Although many barriers concerning the rigidity of ecclesiastical procedures have been broken during recent years, certain customs have nevertheless to be observed. One very important one, from the point of view of embroidery, is concerned with liturgical colour. Certain colours have a particular significance in the Church calendar and it is important to understand this before embarking on any embroidery.

White and Gold are usually used for the most magnificent occasions, including All Saints' Day, Christmas, Epiphany, Easter, Ascension, Trinity Sunday, Feasts of Our Lady, and weddings. This significance means they are usually the most lavishly decorated colours and you can use a great deal of gold thread and rich surfaces in the embroidery.

Red is used for Feasts of the Martyrs, Whitsun, and Feasts of the Apostles. This too is usually richly embroidered, although it should not be quite so lavish as the white and gold. For this purpose the red is usually bright. However, a deep red can be used for Passiontide. As this has a different significance it should not be richly treated.

Yellow is sometimes used in the Church of England for the Feast of the Confessors. This again needs a rich treatment.

Green is more or less an everyday colour and is used between Trinity Sunday and Advent, and also during Epiphany. It should not be so lavishly decorated as the colours for special occasions, although some metal thread may be used.

Blue or Violet is used during Advent and for the first four weeks in Lent. Blue is the more usual colour, particularly a shade often called Advent blue, which is a fairly dark greenish-blue. Other shades may also be used, but in view of the colour's significance it is not wise to choose a very pale or brilliant blue. The embroidery should also be fairly restrained in nature. You could perhaps use applied fabrics and coloured threads rather than metallic surfaces.

Purple is used by the Roman Catholic Church as blue is by the Church of England, and should therefore be treated in a similar manner.

Black is for funerals, All Souls' Day, and, in the Roman Catholic Church, for Good Friday. This colour has a very sombre significance and embroidery must consequently be restricted.

Unbleached Linen is sometimes used during Lent. The design is usually stencilled rather than embroidered, although it could be embroidered in simple red stitchery.

Fig. 149   A mitre with patchwork motifs in various types of silk. (Helen Armstrong)

5 Choosing Fabrics

The choice of background fabric is very important for a piece of embroidery; on this the whole success of the work can depend. Both the colour and texture of the fabric are important. The right surface texture can add considerably to the finished work and, equally, the wrong texture can detract considerably from it. It is perfectly possible to produce two pieces of embroidery using exactly the same colours and get two completely different results by using fabrics of totally different textures. The texture of the background fabric should be chosen to give a particular effect or mood, and all other fabrics used should enhance this.

When choosing fabrics for a piece of embroidery, particularly the background fabric, it is important to make your final choice in the church itself. There are two reasons for this, the most important being that colours can change considerably according to the light; fabrics that look good by artificial lighting in a shop may lose all their impact inside a church. Don't forget to test colours by both natural and artificial light in the church. The second reason for selecting fabrics in the building is concerned with texture. Again, a fabric which looks beautiful within the confines of a shop may lose all its texture and look dull and lifeless in a church because of the scale of the building.

The method of selecting fabrics for a piece of embroidery should be as follows:

1 Decide what vestments or furnishings are needed.
2 Decide upon the liturgical colour required.
3 Obtain as many samples of various types of fabric within the required shade as possible. Many shops and stores are very helpful about lending samples if you explain why you need them.
4 Take the fabrics to the church and view them in both natural and artificial light. They should also be viewed from a distance as well as close to, because fabrics that look good at close range do not always appear satisfactory when viewed from further away.

The types of fabric used in ecclesiastical work have changed considerably over the last few years, although there are still firms who manufacture fabrics specially for this purpose.

However, these can be supplemented by some of the exciting and unusual furnishing and dress fabrics available today to obtain a more interesting range of colour and texture.

Fabrics selected for vestments should be reasonably supple and hang well. Some furnishing fabrics will give good results for this, but it is better to use a rayon Dupion or something of that kind rather than a heavy brocade. Several of the better-known furnishing fabric manufacturers produce a good range of fabrics in plain colours which are suitable for backgrounds. Many dress fabrics can also be used, but their width needs to be taken into consideration in order to avoid too many seams.

For hangings and furnishings you can use heavier fabrics which will usually hang more satisfactorily than lightweight fabrics.

Although the light is often dim in a church, it is best to look for fabrics which are fast to light and fairly durable. Many manufacturers give guidance on this so you can take it into consideration when purchasing your fabrics.

It is best to avoid patterned fabrics, particularly brocades for the background fabric, and especially if you are a beginner, as these are difficult to handle successfully. If you do select a patterned fabric, it is very important to fit the design to the pattern so that the two do not conflict. Nothing looks worse than a formal brocade background with a cross placed a few inches away from the centre of the pattern. It is surprising how often this occurs.

Fig. 150   Samples of fabric suitable for ecclesiastical embroidery.

6 Designing

Many people feel that there is a great mystique about design, particularly where ecclesiastical objects are concerned. This inhibits them from trying their own designs and leads to copying of existing designs. However, there is no reason why you should not start afresh and it is often surprising what people can produce if they are only willing to try.

Fig. 151 Motif worked in turquoise and silver on a purple background. Some of the shapes are applied in suède and the embroidery incorporates a variety of silver threads, cords and purls. (Peggy Mills)

Fig. 152 Free-standing *chi rho*. The structure is covered with a variety of fabrics and the texture in the centre is macramé, using various threads. (Catherine Clift)

There are a number of points which should be remembered when designing, but if they are observed it need not be difficult.

One of the best ways to start is to take some small sample pieces of embroidery into the church and stand back and look at them. The samples might well be some of the experiments with technique described earlier in the book. Usually this has a devastating effect because something which you may have spent several hours lovingly stitching completely disappears in the new setting. However, you will now have learned the most important lesson of all about designing for a church. That is scale. The design must read from a distance. Therefore it has to be bold, almost heraldic or theatrical in concept in order to work. Colour schemes must be striking, as subtle colours blend together and are lost.

If the church is an established one, as most are, you will have to pay attention to the existing furnishings and architectural style. It is no use working for months on something which is ultimately going to clash violently with everything else in the

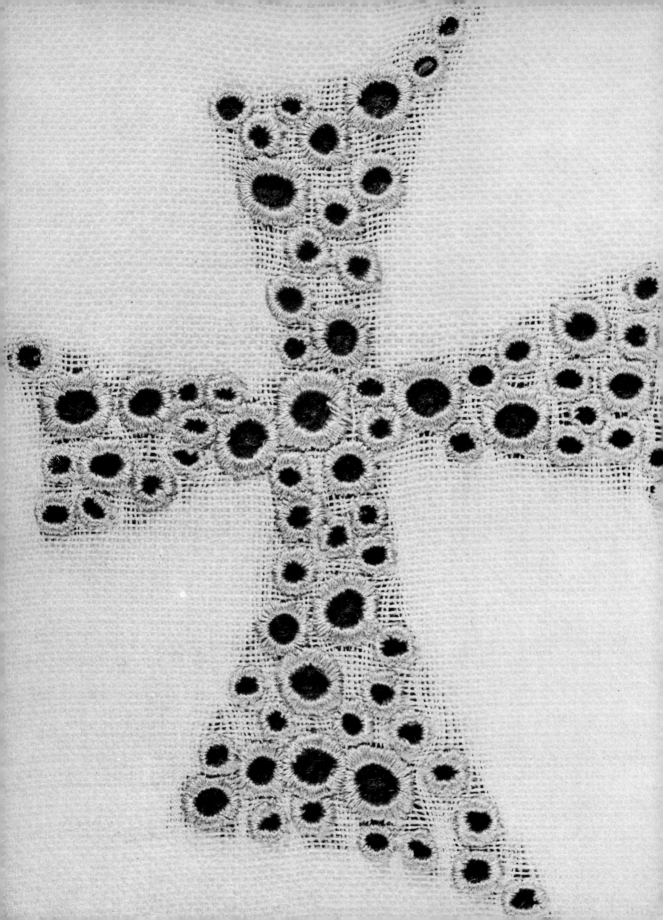

Fig. 153 An irregular cross
worked on a fine white woollen
fabric. The eyelets were worked
on a machine using stitches of
varying widths. The cross is
backed with a contrasting colour.
(Brenda Marchbank)

Fig. 154 Motif in metal threads,
kid, appliqué and beads on blue
woven synthetic straw fabric;
suitable for a burse.
(Lenia Hewitt)

Fig. 155 An unusually short
altar frontal for a modern church,
composed of applied fabrics and
machine embroidery.
(Beryl Patten)

church. However, this does not mean that the new piece of work cannot have an up-to-date design.

Another important point is suitability for purpose. You must consider the type of church architecture and furnishings as well as the liturgical colour. Many people get carried away with the fascination of gold and metal threads and have a great desire to cover everything with them. However, you must remember that you can only do this on the white and red furnishings and vestments. The others must be treated in a more sober fashion, because of their significance. This does not mean to say that the design for the other colours is inferior, just different.

A pictorial approach to design is not fashionable at the moment, the present emphasis being on abstract design. There are, however, several symbols of religious significance which appear time and time again in ecclesiastical embroidery. The cross is the most obvious example of this. Some professional architects and designers decline to make use of such symbols

Fig. 156 Patchwork cross worked in satin ribbons, using shades of one colour together with a few contrasting shades. (Brenda Marchbank)

today but they can often serve as the starting point for a design
(fig. 157) and can be very helpful to those who are less confi-
dent of their own ability and imagination.

The best way to start designing is to have a large quantity of
paper and do lots of small rough drawings with a pencil or
ballpoint pen, always indicating the overall shape of the article
you are designing. Ideally, you should make a scaled down
template of the furnishing or vestment and trace round it a
number of times. You can then start designing within the
right shape (fig. 158).

After you have worked out your ideas you can select the
most interesting ones and work out various colour schemes. It
is a good idea to paint in the background fabric colour if
possible as it will be easier to visualize the completed design.

From various colour combinations select the most promis-

Fig. 157

ing ones. Make a full-scale pattern of the furnishing or vestment on cheap paper. Draw out your design on this and make minor alterations where necessary. Paint it, adding details which might not have been possible on a small scale and making alterations if the scale has affected the design. Crayons and other media can be used to give various textural effects.

When you have finished the full-scale designs take them to the church and look at them *in situ*. They should be viewed at various distances to get the best idea of the impact of the design. If you are making a vestment, it is helpful to pin the design on someone in order to see what it will look like when it is worn.

Make any necessary adjustments.

Your design is now a working drawing.

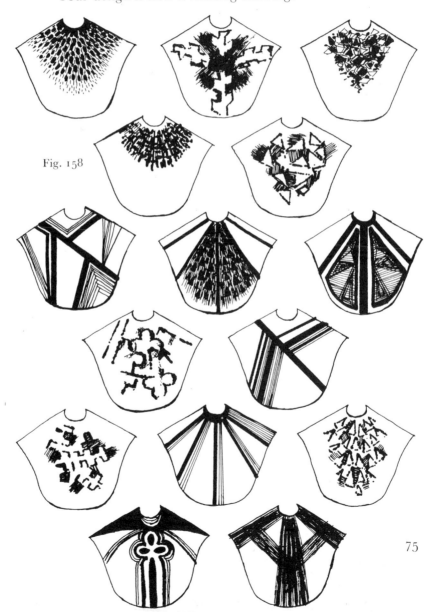

Fig. 158

75

7 Cutting out and Transferring the Design

The first stage of making the actual vestment or furnishing is to cut out the required shapes from the background fabric. If the design was drawn up full size as suggested, you should have no difficulty in making a pattern at this stage. If not, you should draw up the design before making a pattern.

All fabrics should be thoroughly pressed, with a damp cloth or steam iron, if appropriate. The fabric should be absolutely flat before you cut out. Take care not to stretch the fabric with the iron by rubbing it too hard across the surface, which can cause problems when you come to make the work up. If you use a damp cloth or steam iron, leave the fabric flat on a table or clean floor until all the moisture has dried out.

Working on a large, flat surface, pin your pattern onto the fabric and baste around the edge with a contrasting thread. Basting is more permanent than tailor's chalk. If you cut the pattern without seam allowances the basting will be a useful and accurate way of indicating where the edge of the embroidery is to be, and will also act as a stitching line when you make up the article.

Don't forget to leave adequate seam allowances when you cut out; this is vital. At this stage it is always better to leave too much material rather than too little. This applies particularly when you are going to use machine embroidery, as the fabric always shrinks somewhat during machining.

Before basting round the shapes, make sure you have used the correct grain of the fabric and that you are going to cut each piece on the same way of the fabric. The practice of reversing some pattern pieces in order to economize on fabric is dangerous, especially when working with shiny or pile fabrics, as there is often a marked difference in colour, particularly from a distance, if pieces are cut different ways.

When you have cut out the pieces, you can transfer the design for the embroidery. The easiest and most permanent method of doing this is to trace the design from the full-scale painting, making any necessary adjustments. Ballpoint or felt tip pens are probably the most suitable media for tracing. Pencil is not advisable, particularly if you are working on a light-coloured fabric, as it can mark the material and is difficult to remove. Tracing paper is the most suitable paper for tracing, although greaseproof paper, which is less transparent, can be used if the design is sufficiently bold.

It is not necessary to trace every small detail, only the main shapes and directions. If the shapes are to be achieved by applying a fabric to the background, details or small shapes superimposed at this stage will be obliterated. Any small details can be traced in a similar fashion later, during the actual working of the embroidery.

Another reason for not tracing small details at this stage is because it may be necessary to make some adjustments to them as the embroidery progresses. This can arise from working the stitches and often if you copy a painted design slavishly the embroidery becomes dull and uninteresting instead of developing a lively, spontaneous quality.

When you have traced the main features, pin the tracing paper onto the background material in the correct position for the embroidery. Make sure that it is held firmly in place.

Choose a cotton of a contrasting colour and baste through the traced lines onto the fabric, taking care to oversew stitches at the beginning and end of a piece of thread. Your stitches should be small enough to indicate any slight changes in line. When you have finished basting the design, tear away the tracing paper carefully, leaving the stitches still in the fabric.

There are two other methods of transferring a design, but both produce a less durable result and one is rather tedious. However, they are both suitable for small areas of embroidery.

Pricking and pouncing is a laborious, traditional method of transferring a design. First, trace the design on tracing paper and then prick it with a pin, making the holes very close together. Place the design on the fabric and pin it in position. Dust the tracing with powdered chalk or charcoal, whichever will show up best on your background fabric, making sure that it goes through the holes.

When you remove the tracing, the design should be visible in the form of a series of dots. Using white or black water-colour paint, depending on whether chalk or charcoal was used for dusting, join up the dots by painting in the design with a continuous fine line. Be careful when handling the fabric because the paint has a tendency to flake off.

Carbon paper can also be used to transfer a design in certain instances. Trace the design in the usual way and place carbon paper face downwards on top of the fabric, sandwiched in between the fabric and the tracing paper. Trace over the design with a pencil or ballpoint pen and the design will be transferred to the fabric through the carbon paper. Various coloured carbons are available if the normal blue or black is is not suitable.

The main problem with this method is that the carbon has a tendency to rub off onto the fabric in other areas. This can be difficult to remove if the fabric is very light in colour.

8 Stretching a Frame

The next stage depends a great deal on which embroidery techniques you are going to use. If the techniques can be worked in the hand, it is better to do so. The method of framing described below is not suitable for machine embroidery.

When the work is to be done on a frame (fig. 159), it is important to choose a frame which is not too wide, so that your arm can reach underneath to the middle of the embroidery. Only the area to be embroidered needs to be stretched on the frame; the rest of the fabric can be carefully rolled in tissue paper and tacked or pinned round the edge of the frame, so that it does not get in the way.

There are various types of frame available and it is important to choose one which is suitable for your purpose. For small pieces or areas of embroidery a 24-inch (61-cm) or 27-inch (69-cm) rotating frame or threaded side hand frame is perhaps the most satisfactory. These are, however, more suitable for individual work than for group work.

For group work a much longer frame of approximately 4 feet (1.22 m) or more in length is best. This can be rested on tables or trestles, or balanced between two supports. These large frames are of a similar construction to the smaller ones.

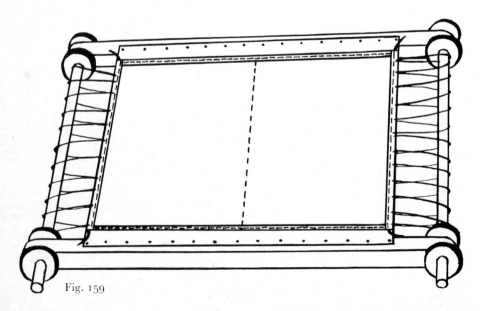

Fig. 159

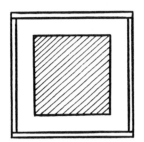

Fig. 160

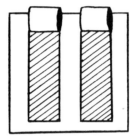

Fig. 161

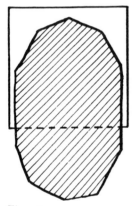

Fig. 162

Fig. 163

If a large frame is difficult to obtain, it is possible to make one, but it must be sufficiently well constructed to withstand both the strain and the weight of embroidery without warping.

Although there are different types of frame, the method of preparing them for embroidery is more or less the same.

The fabric to be embroidered is not usually stretched directly onto a frame because it could be damaged very badly. A backing material of some kind is usually stretched first and the fabric which is to be embroidered is then fixed to it. In the case of ecclesiastical embroidery, unbleached calico or linen is usually used for the backing. Unless the work is very delicate, a medium weight of either fabric is the most suitable. Calico is much cheaper than the more traditional linen and, unless the work is very special, or is intended to last for a considerable time, it is the best material to use.

Begin by cutting the calico to the required size. This is usually determined by the size of the embroidery or by the maximum size of the frame. If the area to be embroidered is small, you do not need the maximum area afforded by the frame. Cut the calico a little larger than the area of the embroidery in order to have some space around the work to take ends through and also perhaps to try out some stitching before you start embroidering. In addition to this, allow approximately an extra $\frac{3}{4}$ inch (19 mm) on each side for turnings (fig. 160).

If the article to be embroidered is larger than the frame, you must take into account the size of the area of embroidery. Often this will go on a frame when the whole article will not, as, for example, with a stole (fig. 161). There is no need to stretch any of the fabric which you are not going to embroider, as it can be rolled in tissue paper for protection and fixed on one side of the frame to keep it in place so that it does not interfere with the embroidery process.

However, should the area of embroidery be larger than the frame, you will have to divide it into areas and complete one area at a time (fig. 162). When you have done one area you can take the embroidery off the frame, stretch another piece of calico and replace the work on the frame, exposing another area for embroidery. Repeat this process until you have finished all the embroidery. If you have to adopt this method of working, make sure the fabric which is not on the frame is always wrapped carefully in tissue paper for protection as described earlier.

When you remove the embroidery from the frame, cut away the calico or linen backing close to the edge of the embroidery before you place another area on the frame (fig. 163). This is necessary in order not to end with several layers of calico in the middle of the work.

When working in this manner it is usual to put the maximum amount of calico on the frame, provided it is not so big that you cannot reach the middle of the work underneath. Cut the backing material about $1\frac{1}{2}$ inches (38 mm) larger on each side than the area you need for working. The backing should be square, which means cutting it along the thread.

Find the exact middle across the fabric and baste a line to mark it along the thread. Fold a double hem along the long edges about $\frac{1}{2}$ inch (13 mm) deep. This should be at right angles to the basting line. The hem should be folded very accurately and pressed, but not stitched (fig. 164).

Find the middle of the webbing and mark it with a pencil or ballpoint pen. Place the backing material on the webbing with the hem uppermost, overlapping it by about $\frac{3}{4}$ inch (19 mm). Line up the centre of the webbing and the tacking line on the material and pin the fabric firmly in position. Working from the centre outwards, pin the hem to the webbing, making sure that it is absolutely straight (fig. 165). Usually the webbing has a herringbone weave; the changes in direction form a straight line which can be useful as a guide.

When you have pinned the hem in position, fix the webbing and basting material together with a back stitch, starting in the centre and working outwards to the last $\frac{1}{2}$ inch (13 mm), which should be left free (fig. 166). The stitching should be done in a strong thread, such as coton à broder, and the stitches can be quite large. You start in the middle to prevent puckering, which might otherwise occur.

Repeat the same process for the other side.

Cut two pieces of string about 3 inches (7.5 cm) longer than the raw edge of the fabric. Lay the string on the fabric with an equal projection at each end, and fold the fabric over it to form a single hem about $\frac{1}{2}$ inch (13 mm) deep. This should be done very accurately and pinned in position. Stitch along both sides using a strong thread and running stitch to hold the string in position (fig. 167).

Put the side pieces of the frame in position, tightening the fabric but not stretching it to its limit at this stage (fig. 168).

Take a very long piece of string and lace over the side pieces of the frame and through the fabric in front of the string (fig. 169). The string strengthens the edge of the fabric as it takes quite a lot of strain when the fabric is fully stretched.

When you have finished lacing, leave about 18 inches (46 cm) extra string at both ends. Repeat the process on the other side. Tighten up the lacing and finish each end off by tying it firmly over the corners of the frame. Do not tie it so tightly that it is impossible to get it undone again because you will need to be able to tighten it again if it becomes slack through pressure when working. The frame is now ready to take the fabric to be embroidered.

Find the exact middle of the background fabric for the embroidery and mark it with a basting line. Place this basting line immediately on top of the basting line on the backing

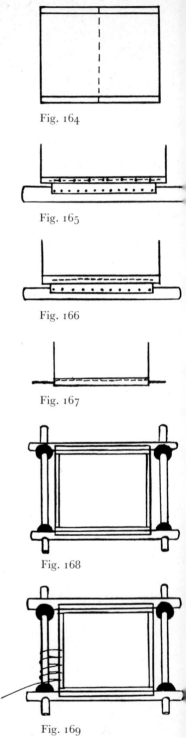

Fig. 164

Fig. 165

Fig. 166

Fig. 167

Fig. 168

Fig. 169

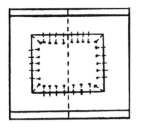

Fig. 170

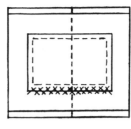

Fig. 171

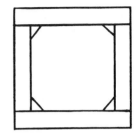

Fig. 172

material. Make sure that the grains of both the fabrics match at this stage; if they do not, the work could pucker when taken off the frame. Working from the centre outwards, pin the fabric onto the backing, making sure that it is absolutely flat (fig. 170). Baste the fabric in position and herringbone around the edge so that it is firmly held (fig. 171). Tighten up the frame so that it is really taut.

If you need to stretch the embroidery temporarily for some purpose, it is not necessary to put it on the type of frame already described. A much simpler arrangement can be devised by fixing four pieces of wood together, making sure that the corners are at right angles and that the wood is strong enough to take the weight and strain of the embroidery without warping (fig. 172). The result is rather like a painting stretcher and the work is stretched in position with drawing pins, either with or without a calico backing.

For machine embroidery use an embroidery ring.

9 Working the Design

When you have experimented with a variety of techniques and have evolved a design, there are one or two points to take into consideration before you start the embroidery. They apply particularly to vestments and to some extent to furnishings.

If the embroidery is designed to last – and if it has a great deal of gold it should be – the techniques used must be reasonably practical. Vestments are, of course, made to be worn and in fact receive quite a lot of wear; they are not always handled as carefully as they might be. This means that everything needs to be sewn down firmly. Long threads floating on top of the material will soon catch and get broken. The same will happen to pieces of gold which are only fixed at one end. Altar linen

Fig. 173 Detail of embroidery using architectural shapes, worked on a purple background. Some of the applied shapes are in suède and kid and the detail has been achieved with a variety of cords and metal thread. (Betty Mayes)

Fig. 174 Panel intended for use in a church, composed of simple patchwork in rainbow colours with applied lettering. (Jain Wright)

has to be laundered and must therefore be even more durable than vestments. Therefore it is important to choose your techniques carefully. This does not mean to say that the embroidery must be dull. It need not be, but you must be sensible.

Any appliqué or padding in the design should be done first. Machine embroidery, if used, should also be done fairly early as it is difficult to put an article with hand embroidery on it into an embroidery ring. Work bold areas of stitching next, and leave the finer details to last.

Canvas work should be started in the middle of the area to be worked. This helps to prevent inequalities in design occurring in the centre, if you have not worked out the design accurately.

If the article to be embroidered has a seam, work the embroidery to within ½ inch (13 mm) of the seam line, leaving a small area along the seam to be completed when the pieces are joined together, or join the seam first and work the embroidery over it. If the seams are at an angle, as shoulder seams are, it is usual to work the embroidery first and join them later. If the embroidery is to be done by a number of people it is usually easiest to work the embroidery first. Otherwise, it is best to join the seams before you embroider.

When embroidery has to be joined make sure that the design will join accurately before you start. This needs to be checked constantly because lines can easily move slightly during working and nothing looks worse than two lines which are meant to join just missing each other. This also applies to shapes.

It is a good idea to disguise joins as much as possible by placing small shapes and a lot of embroidery over them.

10 Making up

You should take as much care when making up a vestment or furnishing as you take with the embroidery. How disappointing it is to see a beautiful piece of embroidery completely ruined by bad craftsmanship during the making up process.

There is nothing particularly difficult about making up. Common sense and sufficient care and attention are all that you need to obtain a satisfactory result. Similar techniques are required for all articles.

Pay special attention to linings, particularly for vestments, as linings are usually visible when they are being worn. It is advisable not to use cheap lining materials, as you really do notice the difference. If the lining is a different colour from the main fabric, make sure that the edges match exactly and the lining does not show on the right side. Both the texture and quality of the lining should be chosen to enhance the design. A very effective use can be made of contrasting colours.

Furnishings

Altar frontals
The method of making up an altar frontal of whatever type is the same as that described for dossals and banners on page 88. Sailcloth, cotton duck or deck-chair canvas may be used as an interlining.

Various methods of suspension have already been described; the section for the top of the altar is attached to the frontal after it has been made up. This must be done very firmly as frontals are heavy and the seam joining the two pieces takes a great deal of strain in both directions.

Altar-cloths
When making up an altar-cloth the treatment of the hem is important, and can make a useful contribution to the design. An ordinary hem is the most straightforward treatment but this is not entirely satisfactory. However, if there is a great deal of embroidery, it may be necessary to use it, as other methods may be too decorative. Hem stitching gives a more finished look to a piece of embroidery provided the embroidery

is not too free in design; this stitch relies on regular spacing and it can appear very rigid.

Allow the width of the hem and an additional $\frac{1}{4}$ inch (6 mm) extra on each side. Spread out the fabric and measure twice the width of the hem, plus $\frac{1}{4}$ inch (6 mm) from each edge. Mark with a pin. Lift with the tip of a pin and pull one thread in each direction until they meet at the corners. Snip the thread at the intersections and remove these threads. Remove as many more as you have to, to make a decorative edge to the hem. These threads should be removed from inside the first thread, and not from the outer edge. Fold back $\frac{1}{4}$ inch (6 mm) around the edges. Fold over again until the edge of the hem meets the outside edge of the withdrawn threads. Mitre the corners (fig. 175) and slip stitch.

Work the stitch wrong side uppermost. Slip the thread inside the hem and bring the needle out at the left-hand corner, about two threads down from the edge. Take the thread diagonally across, behind the first two threads in the area where others have been withdrawn. Bring the needle out and take the thread across the front of the two threads and insert it vertically two threads from the edge to start the next stitch (fig. 176).

There are various other, more complicated, methods of finishing a hem, but they tend to detract from the embroidery.

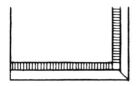

Fig. 175

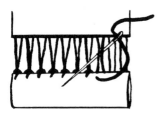

Fig. 176

Fig. 177 Burse in red felt. Strips of felt enriched by machine embroidery and various ribbons and braids have been woven together to form the decoration, which has been enhanced by the addition of some purls. (Carolyn Clarke)

Burses

Cut four 9-inch (23-cm) squares of medium-weight cardboard. The two squares used for the lining can be in a thinner card.

If the embroidery has no backing, stretch a piece of unbleached calico over the outer boards in order to give the edges of the burse a slightly rounded look. The boards for the lining should also have calico or linen stretched over them, as lining materials are often thin.

To stretch the fabric over the card, place the fabric face downwards on a flat surface and put the card in position on top of it (fig. 178). The straight grain of the fabric should coincide with the straight edge of the card. Pin the fabric in position through the ends of the card (fig. 179).

Take a long piece of strong thread, which is not too thick, and, starting in the middle of one side, lace backwards and forwards across the card (fig. 180). The lacing should be spaced at intervals of about ¾ inch (19 mm). Tighten up the thread but keep the card flat. Finish off the ends by oversewing. Fold the corners over neatly and cut away any bulk. Lace the remaining two sides in the same manner (fig. 181) and finish off the ends. Stretch the front and back linings of the burse in a similar manner.

Cut a small strip of background fabric and a small piece of lining approximately 10 × 1½ inches (25 × 3.8 cm). Put right sides together and stitch along the two short sides ½ inch (13 mm) from the edge. Trim the seams and turn them inside. The strip should now be 9 inches (23 cm) long, the same size as the burse. This will form a hinge to join the back and front pieces together.

Place the back and front pieces side by side face downwards, remembering that the top of the design goes towards the hinge. Place the hinge over the two pieces and stick firmly in position (fig. 182).

When the glue is completely dry, place the stretched lining pieces back to back with the back and front sections, and sew the front to the back as invisibly as possible. You may like to finish it with a cord.

The hinge should be made as narrow as possible because it makes the burse look neater. It can be completely eliminated, provided the fabrics are not too bulky; the back and front can simply be stitched firmly together. This method, however, does not wear as well.

Fig. 178

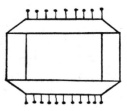

Fig. 179

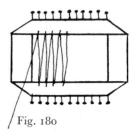

Fig. 180

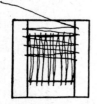

Fig. 181

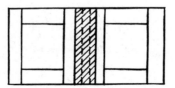

Fig. 182

Fig. 183 Banner dedicated to St James at Dundas, Ontario, Canada, composed of a variety of fabrics and nets applied by machine. (Dorothy Gregson)

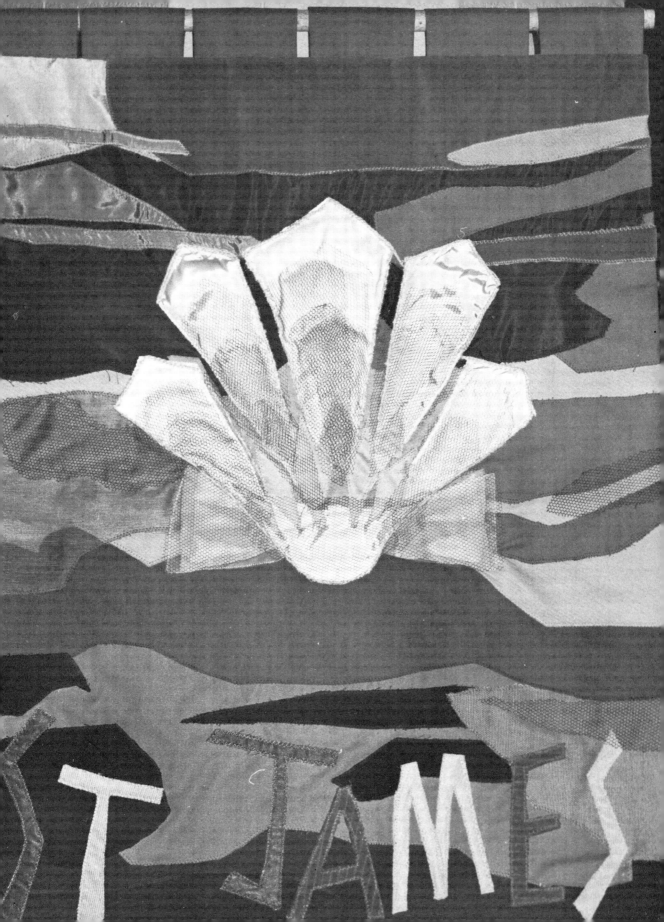

Dossals and banners

These two articles are grouped together because the methods of making them up are virtually the same.

When you have finished the embroidery, mark the centre vertical and horizontal lines by basting. Take care not to damage the embroidery.

Select the material for the interlining. This can be tailor's canvas, deck-chair canvas, or unbleached calico. Sailcloth is also suitable for heavy pieces. Mark the centres of the interlining in the same way as the embroidery, and cut it out. It should be very slightly smaller than the finished article.

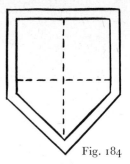

Fig. 184

Place the embroidery face downwards on a flat surface. Lay the interlining on top, matching up the centres (fig. 184). Pin in position, working from the centre outwards, but be careful once again not to damage the embroidery.

Fold over the turnings and tack in position (fig. 185). Mitre the corners. For convex and concave curves, slash the turnings and if necessary remove wedge-shaped sections so that the turnings will lie flat. Check that the work is flat by lifting it and looking at the right side. Make any necessary adjustments.

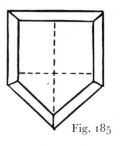

Fig. 185

Catch stitch or herringbone the turnings to the interlining without letting the stitches appear on the right side of the embroidery (fig. 186). It is best to work from the top down the sides, leaving the bottom until last.

If the embroidery is large or very heavy, it is a good idea to attach it to the interlining by a series of tiny stitches worked from the back at regular intervals. The stitches should be virtually invisible from the front, but appear long on the back. This helps to prevent sagging which might occur when the article is hung.

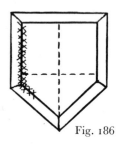

Fig. 186

Make tabs for suspension from strips of the background fabric. Fix the interlining in the same way as that of the main part of the dossal or banner. Line these strips with the material to be used for the lining. The width and length of the strips is variable and depends on the design. When they are finished, attach the tabs firmly to the back of the top edge of the dossal or banner (fig. 187).

Cut the lining with approximately $\frac{1}{2}$-inch (13-cm) turnings and mark both the horizontal and vertical centres with basting. Place the lining in position on the back of the article. Match up the centres and pin. Smooth the lining outwards from the centre and pin in position. Starting from the top edge fold in the necessary amount of material to make the lining and the embroidery equal. Pin in position again. Leave the bottom until last.

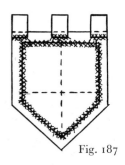

Fig. 187

When you have turned in and pinned all the edges, slip stitch them carefully. If the article to be lined is very large, the lining is quite likely to sag, so catch it with small stitches to the interlining. To do this, match up the centres, and pin. Fold back the lining and catch it through the interlining with

88

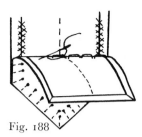
Fig. 188

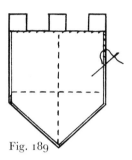
Fig. 189

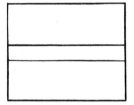
Fig. 190

tiny stitches in a matching thread. The stitches should be well spaced and the stitches on the interlining will therefore be long (fig. 188). Start and finish about 3 inches (7.5 cm)from the edges. Turn in the edges as above and slip stitch (fig. 189).

Pulpit falls
Make up and line the hanging part, following the method described for dossals and banners. The top edges, however, should not be turned in.

Cut a piece of hardboard and a piece of card the same size as the stand. Take care to make the corners of both of these square. Cover the hardboard with a piece of background fabric by the lacing method described for burses. Cover the card with lining, using the same method.

If the pulpit fall is secured with elastic, place the elastic across the front of the lining piece, fold the ends onto the back of the board and stick firmly in position (fig. 190). A wide elastic is generally used; its position depends on the stand but it usually goes in the middle.

Place the two wrong sides of the rectangles together and pin. Stitch on three sides. Tuck the top edge of the hanging section between the two boards on the open side, matching up the fabrics (fig. 191). Slip stitch the hanging section to the board (fig. 192). Reverse and treat the lining in the same way.

Kneelers
There are two basic methods of making up a modern kneeler, both of which depend on the way in which the kneeler was designed.

If you designed the embroidery as one piece, cut the canvas away from the embroidery, leaving approximately $\frac{3}{4}$ inch (19 mm) for turnings (fig. 193). Fold the gussets inwards and work a row of long-armed cross stitches over the fold (fig. 194).

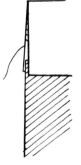
Fig. 191

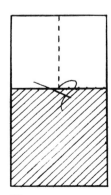
Fig. 192

Fig. 193

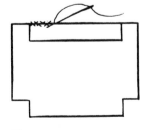
Fig. 194

Fig. 195

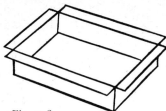

Fig. 196

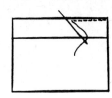

Fig. 197

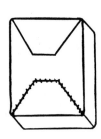

Fig. 198

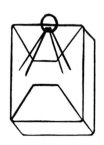

Fig. 199

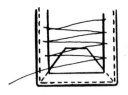

Fig. 200

Sew the corners together and cover with the same stitch (fig. 195). The kneeler should now look like a box (fig. 196).

If the embroidery was made up of five pieces, cut them out, leaving at least $\frac{1}{2}$ inch (13 mm) all round for turnings. Fold the edges of the canvas over onto the wrong side. Place the edge of the gusset together with that of the top of the kneeler, right sides outwards, and stab stitch with buttonhole thread (fig. 197). Make sure you match the thread and the pattern. Join the corner seams in the same way. This should also resemble a box at this stage.

Place a piece of carpet underlay face downwards in the kneeler. Plastic foam or foam rubber can be used for the padding, but it is important to find a material with a suitable density, or the kneeler will disintegrate after a while. The padding can be cut to the correct size by the manufacturer. Wrap a section of padding in a piece of hessian (burlap) and sew the ends firmly (fig. 198).

If the kneelers are to hang, brass curtain rings may be used. Fold a yard (1 m) of tape in half and put one end through the ring. Place the curtain ring in the centre of the top end, largely projecting beyond the kneeler. Cut the loop and spread out the ends of the tape in a fan shape (fig. 199). Sew the tapes firmly to the back of the kneeler pad. This will help to distribute the weight when hanging.

You can use fabric tabs for hanging kneelers but rings are easier and more durable.

Place the pad inside the kneeler and pack any odd corners with Dacron wadding to ensure a tight fit. If you do not do this the kneeler will soon sag when in use. Fold the edges of the canvas over the pad and neaten the corners so that they are not bulky. Lace the sides with string (fig. 200).

Cut a piece of upholsterer's linen or a similar, durable fabric for the backing, leaving approximately 1 inch (25 mm) for turnings. Turn in the edges and pin the backing over the pad, keeping it straight and taut. Stitch it neatly in position with a strong thread (fig. 201).

90

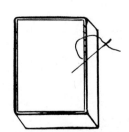

Fig. 201

Carpets

Embroidered carpets need a backing material of some kind, preferably one which is non-slip. They are quite simple to make up.

Place the work face downwards on a flat surface and fold the turnings back. Pin on the backing like a lining, starting from the centre and working outwards. Catch the backing to the front at regular intervals if the carpet is large. Fold in the edge of the backing so that it corresponds with the edge of the embroidery, and slip stitch.

Vestments

Chasubles

Place both the front and back on a flat surface face downwards.

Cut out the interlining, if you need one, without turnings. It is advisable to use a light, soft fabric for this purpose, such as butter muslin, otherwise the garment will become stiff and heavy.

Fig. 202

Mark the centre front and centre back on the interlining and match them to the front and back of the chasuble. Working outwards from the centre, smooth out the interlining and attach it at intervals to the back of the embroidery. This must be done as invisibly as possible. Fold back the turnings, taking care not to stretch those that are on the cross. Slash the hem where necessary and remove wedge-shaped pieces (fig. 202). Pin and baste in position. Catch stitch or herringbone to the interlining, or to the back of the material if you are not using an interlining, taking care that the stitches do not show through on the right side (fig. 203).

Mark the centre back and centre front of the lining, making sure that the grain of the fabric is correct. Cut the lining with generous ½-inch (13-mm) turnings. Match up the centre lines with those of the interlining and pin. Starting from the centre smooth outwards and pin at intervals, keeping all the pins in the same direction (fig. 204). Baste the lining in position, taking care not to damage the embroidery.

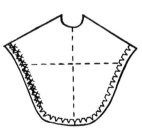

Fig. 203

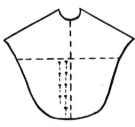

Fig. 204

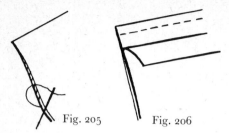

Fig. 205   Fig. 206

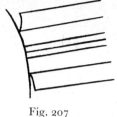

Fig. 207

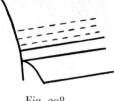

Fig. 208

Fig. 209

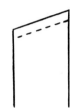

Fig. 210

Fold in the hem so that the edge of the lining and the edge of the embroidery meet exactly. Slash where necessary so that the lining lies flat. Slip stitch the embroidery and the lining together (fig. 205). The stitching should finish roughly 3 inches (7.5 cm) from the shoulder seam, which should be left open.

Fold back the lining. Place the right sides of the back and front together. Match up the shoulder seam, pin and stitch (fig. 206). Press the seam open (fig. 207). Turn up the section of hem over the seam and catch stitch, cutting away any bulk.

Lay out flat again, face downwards. Bring the back lining over the seam and fold a hem in the front lining to coincide with the seam line. Place this over the back lining, pin and baste in position (fig. 208).

Carefully hem stitch the seam in matching thread, letting the stitches penetrate the front and back turnings, but not the right side of the chasuble (fig. 209).

Finish off the neck and shoulder edges with slip stitch.

Copes
Copes are made up in the same way as chasubles, described above. Position the morse when the interlining is in place. Fix the morse firmly in position and take the lining over it.

Stoles
Join the centre back seam, which should be slightly sloping to give some shape (fig. 210). Work a cross or motif over the seam (fig. 211). This can be done in the hand or in a small frame.

Cut two pieces of interlining (dowlas and holland are suitable materials), making them very slightly smaller than the finished shape of the stole, except at the centre back where each piece should be cut about 2 inches (5 cm) longer. It is important to ensure that the grain of the interlining is the same as that of the stole.

Place the stole flat on a suitable surface, face downwards. Put the pieces of interlining in position. Starting at the ends, pin and smooth towards the neck, allowing the pieces to overlap (fig. 212). Pin and baste.

Fig. 211

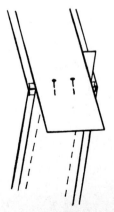

Fig. 212

92

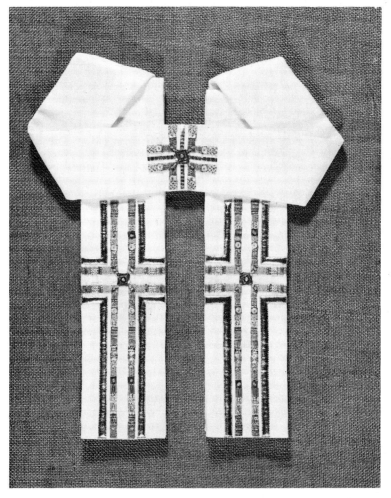

Fig. 214

Shape the neckline by making it into a slight curve, which
will fit neatly around the neck (fig. 214).

Cut the interlining so that the edges meet over the centre
back seam, and stitch them together. Fold the turnings of the
stole over the interlining and catch stitch or herringbone,
starting with the ends and working towards the neck.

Cut two pieces of lining with seam allowances, matching up
the grain with that of the stole. Stitch the centre back seam at
exactly the same angle as that of the stole. Press open.

Match the two centre back seams. Working outwards
towards the ends, pin and baste the lining in place down the
middle of the stole, taking care not to damage the embroidery.

Again starting from the centre back, fold in the turnings so
that the lining is fractionally smaller than the edge of the stole.
Slash where necessary. Slip stitch in position, starting from the
centre back.

Amices
Turn a neat hem in the linen rectangle and attach the tapes on
the wrong side. The tapes are usually about 60 inches (1.52 m)
long. Remember that it may not be necessary to make a new
amice, as there may be existing ones which are suitable.

Apparels
When you have finished the embroidery, trim round the edge,
leaving approximately ½ inch (13 mm) all round for turnings.

Cut the interlining exactly the same width and slightly
shorter than the finished length. Mark the centre of the apparel
and the centre of the interlining. Attach the centres, keeping
the apparel slightly bent, so that the embroidery is on the outer
curve (fig. 215). This will help the embroidery to lie more
satisfactorily around the neck. Turn the edges of the embroidery over the interlining, pin and baste in position. Catch
stitch it to hold it in place.

Cut out the lining. Keep it taut and hem it as invisibly as
possible.

The apparel should be attached to the amice in such a
manner that it can be unpicked easily for laundering purposes.

Fig. 215

11 Group Projects

Where a set or a number of vestments are needed, or perhaps one very large article, such as a Laudian altar frontal or dossal, carpet or kneelers, it is preferable to turn the embroidery into a group project rather than let it be the work of one individual. This can save a considerable amount of time and can also generate a great feeling of comradeship amongst members of the congregation if the project is properly organized.

In order to begin it is necessary to appoint someone who has enough ability to direct the project satisfactorily. This involves both a knowledge of technique and the ability to deal with people. Some churches, where projects of this nature have been undertaken, have consulted the church architect on design problems and allowed him to make the final decisions on the most suitable designs for embroidery. This can be of considerable help. However, for those churches unable to consult an architect or designer for various reasons, the project organizer must take rather more responsibility for design, consulting of course with the vicar.

If the group is meeting for the first time, it is a good idea to give the members time to get to know each other and to discover the various standards of technical ability within the group before they embark on a large undertaking. The charming old lady and the enthusiastic young wife may not know one end of the needle from the other when it comes to stitching, whereas the rather shy, retiring member of the group may be a superb needlewoman. These things are not immediately obvious.

A good way to begin is with experiments involving some of the techniques which might be used in the project, such as those discussed at the beginning of this book. Provided it does not go on too long, this introductory period can be very useful and help things to run smoothly later. From preliminary experiments the group organizer can deduce a number of things. Firstly, she can ascertain the technical standard of the group. This is very important because it is no use embarking on a project which is to have a lot of very delicate gold work if the group produces work which looks as if it has been stitched with a meat skewer. The experiments should give the organizer some indication of the type of embroidery the group could use.

Another important point is to observe the groups people fall

95

into naturally during that period. They usually elect to be near a person they like or with whom they feel some sympathy or understanding. After a few weeks these patterns will probably sort themselves out and it is a good idea to make a note of them so that as far as possible people can be asked to work with others with whom they have a good relationship. Relationships are a very important factor in the group organization because if two people who are antagonistic to each other are asked to work on the same piece of embroidery there will be a constant battle between them throughout the project. This could ruin what would otherwise be an enjoyable experience and might even drive other members of the group away.

When embarking on the project itself, the group organizer must take responsibility for ordering all materials. The orders are usually passed on to the vicar or church treasurer so that the organizer decides on the materials and quantities to be ordered and where they are to be ordered from but does not pay for goods herself. Remember to order everything in good time so that delayed deliveries do not hold you up.

As the organizer has responsibility for the direction of the design project she has to decide on the best method of approach. Everyone should be given the opportunity to try designing. The best designs can then be selected. This is usually more satisfactory than electing one person to design the whole project, although of course some people may prefer to do it that way.

Before you reach the cutting out stage you will have to decide how the work is to be executed; in the hand or stretched on a frame, or perhaps both at various stages. This will dictate to a certain extent how the work is to be divided amongst the group. There are no hard and fast rules about this and the decision depends on a number of factors: the design, the techniques to be used, and the number of people in the group. The final decision on this point must belong to the group organizer. She will also supervise the cutting out and working of the embroidery.

Another point to remember is that the techniques used should be the same on each section of the embroidery. It is no use having one pair of embroiderers doing one thing and another pair doing something totally different on two adjoining sections of the work, which can easily happen if there is no-one to co-ordinate the project; this too is the job of the group organizer.

Ideally, the organizer should not actually do any of the embroidery but should keep an eye on what is going on the whole time. This way mistakes can be avoided and time saved. Some of the responsibility could be delegated if necessary but this should be avoided as far as possible, or you will tend to lose control of the project. Figs. 110, 111, 127, 128, 129, 138 and 139 all show work produced as part of a group project.

12 Towards a New Approach

Fig. 216 A printed mitre in mauve silk with a free style of embroidery using applied shapes, hand stitching and some metal threads. (Regina Arkwright)

Although many people do not realize it, the so-called 'modern' approach to Church embroidery has been around for some time. This embroidery has mainly been produced for our larger churches and cathedrals, but often in a small parish church you can find vestments and furnishings in a contemporary style. It is only right that we should be using up-to-date embroideries

Fig. 218 Banner designed for St James's Church, Dundas, Ontario, Canada. (Gay Walker)

Fig. 217 (Left) Hanging inspired by the story of St Francis. The background is painted with dye and the shapes have been loosely applied with hand stitchery. Suitable for a children's corner. (Julia Jeffries)

in our churches, as many of those left by our forbears have little meaning today, and so often border on the sentimental.

However, many embroideries designed relatively recently also have a dated look. Design ideas which were popular ten or fifteen years ago are still being produced. Is this progress? Concepts within the Church and our way of life have changed considerably since then; should this not be reflected in the work produced for ecclesiastical purposes?

This poses two major questions. Does ecclesiastical embroidery really have to last for generations, and is it necessarily better because it does? If you really think about it, the answer must be no. In the past work has been produced to last but there is no hard and fast rule which says we must do the same. You can become very tired of seeing the same old banners and hangings collecting more and more dust as the years go by.

Obviously, if a great deal of gold thread has been used in a design it should be made to last because it is so expensive. But the design is not necessarily better because it has been worked in gold. Gold is becoming increasingly difficult to obtain and in the future it may be necessary to use other techniques. Why not start now?

One of the major expenses of upkeep, particularly the up-keep of vestments, is cleaning. Consequently, many vestments

99

you never had it... so good...

Fig. 219 Banner designed for St James's Church, Dundas, Ontario, Canada. The hamburger motif is padded and treated in a very three-dimensional way. (Carolyn Beard)

are not cleaned as often as they should be. So, why not use washable fabrics and techniques which will go with them? Many fabrics manufactured today will wash, even if not always in a washing machine. Courtelle is an interesting example, as are mixtures of natural and synthetic fibres. There are some exciting fabrics produced in these ranges if you take the trouble to look for them; they are often very wide, which is another point in their favour. Provided you are careful about what is done with the embroidery, there is no reason why you should not be able to wash all the vestments.

On the other hand, why make them to last at all? This is pure tradition; do we have to follow it? Why not create

Fig. 220 Banner designed by a seven-year-old using simple appliqué shapes. (Kendra Gregson)

something out of relatively cheap materials, let it be worn until it is dirty, and then replace it? This is also perfectly feasible. You can create something just as beautiful out of cheap materials in a day, as you can make using the most expensive silks and spending weeks covering them with gold work. The results are different, but just as valid.

The other major question which arises is concerned with design standards. Does design have to be the preserve of the professional? Even today there is a great mystique about designing for the church, and many people believe that professional designers only should be employed. This is expensive and is one of the major factors inhibiting a widespread use of modern embroidery in our churches. The attitude is understandable of course if a considerable amount of money is to be spent on a piece of embroidery; it is fairly obvious that a professional is likely to do the job better than an amateur. But is this necessarily a good thing, particularly for a small parish church? The professional designer often lives a considerable distance from the parish and is not at all involved with it. His or her work is likely to be executed in a cold and detached manner. This lack of involvement may be reflected in the design, which consequently does little for the church. If a church is to be alive, it must be for the people. Shouldn't the people be able to create something for the church?

Children as well as adults should be able to participate in creating for their church. All too often the furnishings and decoration in children's corners are drab and disappointing. Children must find them very dull, especially after the imaginative approach in schools today. Why not use the same principles and allow them to create something for themselves as an integral part of their religious instruction?

It is perfectly possible for members of even the smallest church to create their own embroidery. As long as they can forget their inhibitions about design and the Church and let the work come from the heart the spontaneity and life in the resulting embroideries would more than make up for their lack of knowledge concerning design. In this way a great many more churches could have exciting hangings and vestments which could be changed from time to time as well as a more lively and involved congregation.

List of Suppliers

Great Britain

Metal threads, cords and braids
Art Needlework Industries Ltd, 7 St Michael's Mansions, Ship St, Oxford
Louis Grosse Ltd, 36 Manchester St, London W1
A. R. Mowbray & Co. Ltd, 28 Margaret St, London W1
Mace & Nairn, 89 Crane St, Salisbury, Wiltshire
The Needlewoman Shop, 146–148 Regent St, London W1R 6BA
Christine Riley, 53 Barclay St, Stonehaven, Kincardineshire, Scotland AB3 2AR
Royal School of Needlework, 25 Princes Gate, London SW7
J. Wippell & Co. Ltd, 11 Tufton St, London SW1
55–56 High St, Exeter
Cathedral Yard, Exeter
24–26 King St, Manchester

Threads
Anchor embroidery threads
The Needlewoman Shop, 146–148 Regent St, London W1R 6BA
D.M.C. threads
Christine Riley, 53 Barclay St, Stonehaven, Kincardineshire, Scotland AB3 2AR
C. & F. Handicraft Supplies Ltd (large quantities only), 346 Stag Lane, Kingsbury, London NW9

Beads, sequins and imitation stones
Cotswold Craft Centre, 59 Little Herberts Road, Cheltenham, Gloucestershire
Ells & Farrier, 5 Princes St, Hanover Square, London W1
Sesame Ventures, Greenham Hall, Wellington, Somerset

Leather, suède, and gold and silver kid
The Light Leather Co., 18 Newman St, London W1

Fabrics
All fabrics
Harrods Ltd, Brompton Road, London SW1
Heal & Son Ltd, 196 Tottenham Court Road, London W1
John Lewis & Co. Ltd, Oxford St, London W1
Liberty & Co. Ltd, Regent St, London W1
Rubans de Paris, 39A Maddox St, London W1
Welsh flannel
Henry Griffiths & Son, Tregwynt Factory, Haverfordwest, Pembrokeshire
Linen
Mary Allen, Turnditch, Derbyshire
Mace & Nairn, 89 Crane St, Salisbury, Wiltshire
The Needlewoman Shop, 146–148 Regent St, London W1R 6BA

Interlinings and haberdashery
John Lewis & Co. Ltd, Oxford St, London W1
MacCulloch & Wallis Ltd, 25–26 Dening St, London W1R 0BH

Plastic foam
Cooper's Plastic Foams Ltd, Stamford Works, Crompton St, Ashton-under-Lyne, Lancashire

United States of America

Metal threads
Bucky King Embroideries Unlimited, 121 South Drive, Pittsburgh, Pennsylvania 15238
Macey's, Fifth Avenue, New York
Tinsel Trading Co., 7 West 36th St, New York, 18

Threads
American Thread Corporation, 90 Park Avenue, New York
Yarn Bazaar, Yarncrafts Ltd, 3146 N St North West, Washington D.C.

Beads
Amar Pearl & Bead Co. Inc., 19001 Stringway, Long Island City, New York
Hollander Bead and Novelty Corporation, 25 West 37th St, New York 18

Leather
Aerolyn Fabrics Inc., 380 Broadway (Corner of White St), New York

All materials for ecclesiastical embroidery
Bucky King Embroideries Unlimited, 121 South Drive, Pittsburgh, Pennsylvania 15238

Bibliography

Church Kneelers by Joan Edwards. Batsford, London, and Branford, Newton Centre, Massachusetts, 1967.
Church Needlework by Beryl Dean. Batsford, London, 1961.
Church Needlework by Hinda M. Hands. Faith Press, London, 8th edition 1961.
Ecclesiastical Embroidery by Beryl Dean. Batsford, London, and Branford, Newton Centre, Massachusetts, 1958.
Ideas for Church Embroidery by Beryl Dean. Batsford, London, and Branford, Newton Centre, Massachusetts, 1968.
Metal Thread Embroidery by Barbara Dawson. Batsford, London, and Taplinger, New York, 1968.
Saints, Signs and Symbols by W. Ellwood Post. S.P.C.K., London, and Morehouse, New York, 1966.

Index

Page numbers in italic type refer to illustrations.